PHILOSOPHY of SCIENCE and RACE

NAOMI ZACK

Routledge
Taylor & Francis Group

NEW YORK AND LONDON

Published in 2002 by
Routledge
29 West 35th Street
New York, NY 10001
www.routledge-ny.com

Published in Great Britain by
Routledge
11 New Fetter Lane
London EC4P 4EE
www.routledge.co.uk

Library of Congress Cataloging-in-Publication data is available
from the Library of Congress.

Philosophy of Science and Race / Naomi Zack
ISBN 0-415-94163-6 — ISBN 0-415-94164-4 (pbk.)

PHILOSOPHY of SCIENCE and RACE

To my (future) grandchildren, and their friends

A man cannot dispel his fears about most matters if he does not know the nature of the universe but suspects the truth of some mythical theory.

—Epicurus, *The Extant Remains, XII*

'Tis Ambition enough to be employed as an Under-Labourer in clearing Ground a little, and removing some of the Rubbish, that lies in the way to Knowledge; which certainly had been very much more advanced in the World, if the Endeavours of ingenious and industrious Men had not been much cumbred with the learned but frivolous use of uncouth, affected, or unintelligible Terms, introduced into the Sciences, and there made an Art of, to that Degree, that Philosophy, which is nothing but the true Knowledge of Things, was thought unfit, or uncapable to be brought into well-bred Company, and polite Conversation. Vague and insignificant Forms of Speech, and Abuse of Language, have so long passed for Mysteries of Science; And hard or misapply'd Words, with little or no meaning, have, by Prescription, such a Right to be mistaken for deep Learning, And height of Speculation, that it will not be easie to persuade, either those who speak, or those who hear them, that they are but the Covers of Ignorance, and hindrance of true Knowledge.

—John Locke, "The Epistle to the Reader,"
An Essay Concerning Human Understanding

Contents

Preface and Acknowledgments

It is now a sign of intellectual sophistication if scholars of race relations and racial experience say something about the lack of a scientific foundation for race. This occurs across liberal arts disciplines, as well as within biology and anthropology, where scientific race studies originated. But in the humanities, particularly, those who easily deny the scientific foundation of race are often in denial about their continued use of concepts that presuppose the kind of racial taxonomy that the missing scientific foundation would have provided. The contemporary scientific issues and data that are relevant to the nonexistence of biological race are cordoned off from humanistic endeavors, as though an exaggeration of their "technicality" were a justification for ignorance or oblivion. Many think that it is enough to say that race is "socially constructed" and then move on to more pressing matters, as though that matter were not the most pressing.

While the full scientific story about the nonexistence of human races does require some patience and concentration to grasp, it does not require any more preparation and training than other subjects about which educated people feel obligated to know something. Still, there is some conceptual analysis that makes the case more plain than if one were to read original sources. And it helps in putting together the plain case if one can be detached from both short-term political concerns and the formidability of science to nonscientists. That is why, as a philosopher, I decided to compose a detailed conceptual account of how the idea of race fails at this time to have support in the relevant contemporary sciences. My contribution is to consider the contemporary science in terms of the main bases for ideas of physical race in common sense and in earlier science: essences, geography, appearance or phenotypes, genetics, and genealogy. It is no coincidence that these same bases used to be accepted as a foundation for race in science—the modern concept of race began in science. By now, science has moved on, but common sense and humanistic scholarship lag by over a century. I hope that anthropologists and biologists, as well as other philosophers, will read the book as a starting point for their own analyses and reflections. If this page happens to be as far as any reader has time to go, let me give away the crux of the matter right here: *It is the taxonomy of human races that science fails to support, not any one or even many of the hereditary traits that society deems racial.*

I began research for the book while on sabbatical leave from the Philosophy Department at the University of Albany, State University of New York, during the fall 1999 semester. I am tremendously grateful to Richard J. Hoffmann, who while dean of the College of Arts and Sciences at the University of Albany from fall 1998 through 2000 encouraged my work on this project and supported my career development beyond it. I will always be indebted to the University at Albany, to the Philosophy Department, specifically, and generally to university President Karen R. Hitchcock and, before her, President H. Patrick Swygert (now president of Howard University), for maintaining an academic environment in which I was able to produce earlier books on the subject of race: *Race and Mixed Race* (1993), *Thinking About Race* (1998), and a book on philosophy of science and seventeenth century identities, *Bachelors of Science* (1996). I view those books, as well as the articles and anthologies I produced during the 1990s, as necessary warm-up for this undertaking. My earlier work on race would not have been possible if Kwame Anthony Appiah had not introduced the scientific problems with race to philosophical racial studies during the early 1990s, and that debt carries over into this project. During the years I have been working on race, I have received much encouragement and support from Laurence Thomas, Philip Kitcher, and J. L. A. Garcia and I want to take this opportunity to express my gratitude to them.

I completed the penultimate draft of the manuscript during the spring semester of 2001, while looking forward to joining the faculty of the Philosophy Department at the University of Oregon in Eugene. It was inspiring to keep in mind that issues addressed here would be relevant to my future work with Ph.D. philosophy students at UO. More than that, now into my second quarter at the University of Oregon, the quality of my experience has thus far surpassed my expectations of a pluralistic philosophy department, with engaged, supportive, and congenial colleagues. As well, I want to thank President Dave Frohnmayer, Senior Vice President and Provost John Mosely, and Executive Assistant to the President David Hubin for their commitment to diversity at the University of Oregon.

Different chapters benefited from audience reaction to earlier drafts. I presented chapter 1, "Philosophical Racial Essentialism: Hume and Kant," to graduate fellows at the Institute on Race and Social Division at Boston University in February 2001 and to the Philosophy Department at the University of Oregon in Eugene in January 2001. I am grateful to Glenn C. Loury, director of the institute, for inviting me to speak there and to Cheyney Ryan, whose colleague I have become, for organizing the Oregon session. The first two-thirds of Chapter 2, "Geography and Ideas of Race," was a paper in a special session arranged by the American Philosophical Association Committee on the Status of Women as part of "Philosophical Explorations of Science, Technology and Diversity," an APA project funded by a grant from the National Science Foundation; the session was held at the Eastern Division Meeting of the American Philosophical Association in New York in December 2000. My thanks to Sandra Harding and Nancy Tuana for inviting me to participate.

Chapter 6, "Race and Contemporary Anthropology," is a revised and shortened version of "Philosophical Aspects of the 1998 AAA Statement on 'Race'," an article published in the December 2001 issue of *Anthropological Theory*. The original version was much improved by Stephen Reyna's editorial guidance and Jonathan Marks's external review comments.

The penultimate version of the manuscript benefited from the two anonymous external reviewers for Routledge, a philosopher and an anthropologist. I am also indebted to John Relethford, who read the penultimate copy in a way that was "geared primarily to the accuracy and completeness of statements regarding human biological variation." Relethford's criticism and recommendations for additional primary sources in biological anthropology, particularly regarding the current *multiregional hypothesis* about the origins of modern humans, have enabled me to attain further scientific literacy as a background for the conceptual analysis I pursue here.

This is the point at which I would be expected to take responsibility for all remaining errors. But there is almost as much confusion about what it means in anthropology as in the humanities and other social sciences to say that race lacks scientific foundation. So, I say that all remaining bona fide mistakes are mine, and I beg the readers across disciplines, as well as philosophers, to focus on the conceptual analysis and broad facts.

I apologize to those of my colleagues in African American philosophy, racial studies, and racial theory if the book creates an impression of slighting their concerns. I take their concerns about racism with the utmost seriousness, and I believe that the concerns I am raising here are part of the same liberatory tradition and the same tradition of uplift. Lucius Outlaw, Tommy Lott, Leonard Harris, Lewis Gordon, Bill Lawson, Jorge Garcia, and Bernard Boxill: Please continue to bear with me. At this time, there are few scholars who are able and interested to consider a philosophical account of the scientific emptiness of race, who are not both liberatory scholars of race and people "of color." Or feminists. I have received some of the most solid support for my work over the past ten years from feminist philosophers. They have been extraordinarily generous in inviting me to speak at American Philosophical Association meeting sessions. Although I have addressed issues of gender, and gender and race together, in other work, and will continue to do so, this book does not directly take up feminist subjects. But I think the past twenty years of feminist philosophy contribute to the possibility of a book like this. My debt to feminist philosophers is therefore substantial, and I believe I am loyal to the same objectives shared by Nancy Tuana, Laurie Shrage, Sandra Harding, Linda Alcoff, Linda Nicholson, and Alison Jaggar, to name a few.

Damon Zucca, my editor at Routledge, expressed continued interest in the manuscript over the two years I worked on it. His philosophical expertise and intellectual engagement are rare in present academic publishing. I will always be grateful for his enthusiasm and stability about my treatment of a subject that is still abandoned to the winds of received opinion.

And finally, my sons Alexander and Bradford are the future, as are my students. It makes it a lot easier to do this kind of work insofar as it is for their sake and the sake of those to whom they will be elders.

NZ
Eugene, Oregon
February 15, 2002

Introduction:
Reason and Method

The motto on the calling card of the hero in the 1950s television Western could be used by philosophers: "Have Gun, Will Travel." Philosophers often assume that they can say something useful about the findings and conclusions of scientists. The importance of science and its public nature invite this scrutiny. Philosophers find science inviting because the primary theories of the modern sciences originated in philosophy and are still familiar to philosophers as part of their own history. Contemporary science is also a live topic for contemporary philosophers.

If a scientific subject is difficult for nonpractitioners to understand, a translation of facts and theories into ordinary prose may be useful to those in other fields, provided there is no distortion or oversimplification. A more exciting philosophical contribution is the analysis of conceptual issues that resolves disputes among scientists and clarifies confusions about the interpretation of data. Philosophers may also defend the findings of science against the superstitions of the public and other nonscientists. If the scientific subject is already contested in social contexts, it may be incumbent upon philosophers to defend the scientific project, as well as the philosophical contribution. A philosopher's work on science may thus be adversarial, skeptical, and unwelcome to many, including other philosophers.

The subject of this book is philosophy of science of race. By "philosophy of science" I mean systematic and logical analysis of the findings and conclusions of scientists. The underlying justification of the scientific enterprise is that, for any given time period, science is the ultimate authority concerning which things are physically real and what their characteristics are. This justification is related to a minimal commitment to philosophical realism, as I will soon explain.

Philosophy of Science of Race

The philosophical tools necessary for philosophy of science of human race are classic. "Race" means a biological taxonomy or set of physical categories that can be used consistently and informatively to describe, explain, and make predictions about groups of human beings and individual members of those groups. The idea of human races has at different times and in different combinations referred to essences, geographical ancestral origins, typological traits such as skin color, heredity, and genealogy, or individual and group lineage. If it is clear what such a typology requires empirically, then it can be determined whether human natural history and present differences support scientific racial taxonomy or whether "race" is scientifically real. In making this determination, it is important to avoid ordinary fallacies of definition and argument, which include: vagueness and vacuity of terms, begging the question, circularity in reasoning, assertion of contradictory statements, arguments from authority, equivocation about what terms mean, and so forth. In addition, there is the empirical constraint that claims or generalizations about biological structures or traits be based on relevant facts, so that they are not merely speculative or metaphysical.

The philosophical process of analyzing scientific findings and conclusions that are relevant to the existence of race proceeds in an ordinary and orderly philosophical way, so that fallacy-avoidance and empirical constraint are applied to relevant scientific information. Such a progression is, I hope, evident in the content of this book. It would be artificial and pedantic to set out the fallacies and empirical constraints beforehand. All that is needed for the analysis to go through is a minimal commitment to logic and empiricism (by me and the reader).

Science and Realism

The ability of science to yield truth about the physical world is taken for granted by scientists and empiricist philosophers. But not all philosophers and other scholars who currently address race as a subject of politics, culture, ethics, identity, and identity politics accept science as a major epistemic authority. Even those who recognize the importance of science for knowledge about physical reality might ask why the findings and conclusions of scientists should be accepted as the ultimate authority about physical reality. Here are three reasons. First, the public thinks that scientists are the ultimate authority about physical reality, and this belief is found in both ordinary and educated opinion. Second, the history of Western science is a development of inquiries about the physical world and its contents. Third, a belief in the existence of an external and objective world leads to the conclusion that the best way to acquire knowledge about this world is through science because of its special methodology.

The belief that the truth about the physical world is ultimately in the possession of scientists has since the 1970s been captured by philosophers in a referential theory of meaning known as the New Theory of Reference. According to W. V. O. Quine, Saul Kripke, Hilary Putnam, and others, the linguistic meaning of folk terms or names for objects in ordinary language are the natural kind terms used by scientists. These natural kind terms, for instance *H20* and other formulas and equations, are the *proper names* (like

Naomi Zack) of entities or relations that exist in the physical world.[1] The public may not know exactly what it is about natural kinds that makes them what they are, but, generally, it is secure in the belief that scientists are in possession of this information about *underlying traits*, and that their terms for them are defining.[2] For example, the public may not understand scientific classifications that preclude calling whales "fish" or spiders "insects," but it accepts their scientific classifications as mammals and arachnids. The public thus has a good grasp of its own ignorance, so that in naming and sorting physical objects, scientists are accepted as the final authorities on naming and sorting, in recognition of their power to name and sort (which results from institutional support and resources). The public thereby has *semantic deference* for the pronouncements of scientists. [3]

The claim that science is the ultimate authority on physical reality because educated people believe it is, is itself an argument from authority. But, there is protection from this fallacy in discussion of race. Race is believed on folk levels to have meaning in science, and that belief is itself part of the folk meaning of race. If race is not scientifically meaningful, then the meaningfulness of race in folk terms is thereby undermined. [4] Thus, the argument from scientific authority is not offered directly in support of a philosophical analysis of race in science, but as part of the content of what is being analyzed. *Race as commonly understood is believed to have an existence vouchsafed by the authority of science.*

Modern science began in the sixteenth and seventeenth centuries with the philosophical work of Bacon, Descartes, Hobbes, and Locke and with the empirical studies of Newton, Boyle, and their cohort. Until the eighteenth century, "natural philosophy," the name for what we now call 'science,' referred to studies of the material world, which were based on and justified by empirical observation.[5] Newtonian physics became the model for subsequent scientific enquiry. Biology, which did not appear in modern form until the late eighteenth century, has always been a naturalistic or materialist science. There has been no effective competitor to the physical sciences for knowledge about the physical world. Even within the social sciences, which did not formally develop until the nineteenth century, the methods and types of conclusions characteristic of the physical sciences were accepted as models for the study of the social and psychological world.

Still, and of course, the history of the physical sciences and their influence does not give us the full story about human history, and it is to a large degree separate from cultural history and the history of ideas. In the twentieth century, critical consternation grew about the awkwardness of that legacy from physical science, according to which social human differences of class, race, and gender were presumed to have biological, that is, physical, foundations. Almost all of the critical work on social class during both the nineteenth and twentieth centuries, and the late twentieth century liberatory scholarship on race and gender, was developed against the grain of the biological legacy from physical science. The general theme of the criticism was and still is that the categories of nonwhite race and nonmale gender do not reflect biological natural kinds that determine and justify diminished social status relative to the categories of white race and male gender. The working hypothesis driving the criticism has been that those aspects of nonwhite race and nonmale gender that are subordinate to aspects of white race and male gender are the result of culture rather than nature. The plausibility of this critical hypothesis would seem to require a background assumption that some aspects of human group difference are not culturally constructed, but physically or biologically real, which is to say, natural, capable of origination without human invention, in need of no special cultural formation for their development, and, universal for *Homo sapiens*. If there were nothing natural about human beings, the claim that this or that about some of them is culturally constructed would not be worth asserting. For instance, those who deny biological foundations for race do not in general deny the existence of human biological differences. Rather, they claim that the *racial* aspects of some of these differences are culturally constructed, and that the 'unconstructed' biological differences associated with race, as it is socially constructed, are small and unimportant.

Some who write about the social construction of gender assert that the categories of male and female sex, as described in the biological sciences and medicine, are also socially constructed.[6] In addition, there is a large amount of philosophy of science literature about the construction of scientific categories in physics and other subjects that are not about human beings.[7] It could be the case that all scientific categories, and not just the malign social ones of nonwhite race and nonmale gender, are constructed, or, in some way "made up" by people. Construction in itself need not entail lack of objectivity or complete lack of reality, especially in social contexts. However, if everything is constructed, then critical theorists of race and gender have the burden of showing why the constructions in which they are interested are worse than other social constructions and, perhaps, as social constructions, worse than the constructions in the physical sciences. Whatever the outcome of that ontological and epistemological project, the task remains to address the fact that the terms 'race' and 'male' and 'female' are commonly assumed to have physical referents that can be studied in the physical sciences. The verified presence of its scientifically accessible referents would make race real (the same can be said of the gender terms, but the subject of this book is race). The analytic, or philosophical, task is to explain the ways in which 'race' lacks scientifically accessible referents, that is, the ways in which race is not real. Once this has been done, it will be evident that race must be a social construction, although questions about how it is constructed and what to do about that construction would still have to answered.

Suppose it can be shown that race is not real in the way the public thinks it is. Another question is whether other things are real in the ways the public, scientists, and some philosophers think that they are. A plausible realist position, even a minimal one, would simplify critiques of false social constructions, by providing criteria for real entities. I think that many things are real in the way people think they are and my minimalist realism amounts to the following.

There is a world that exists independently of thought, sensation, perception, language, and other symbolic representation. Information about characteristics of this world is accessible through the human senses. Similar sensory conditions and sensory equipment result in the same or equivalent symbolic descriptions among different observers. The sensory information thus agreed upon can be combined in agreed-upon ways to result in knowledge. Knowledge, or systems of warranted beliefs, can be used to manipulate what is further observed (by different observers), and it can also be used to predict what will be observed in the future. Objects and events in the world occur in what humans perceive and believe to be regularities. Some of the regularities are more general than others, and descriptions of them may both imply and explain descriptions of less general regularities. In this sense, the regularities are *nomological*, and in some cases, causal. This physical, mind-independent, knowable and regular world is the referent of the phrase 'the real world,' although it is really just "the world.'

In addition to the world, there are possible and probable worlds and states of them. There is a penumbra of valuation accompanying the distinctions between the world on the one hand, and possible and probable worlds, on the other. Given all things equal, the world and its states is better than possible or probable worlds and their states. Knowledge useful to humans pertains to the world, because they are part of it. Although when people falsely believe that something is part of the world, and it isn't, and they act on such belief, their beliefs and actions are indeed part of the world.

My realist position would not be acceptable to all philosophers or members of the public. But, it is close enough to the realism that the public is generally committed to, so that if something believed to be part of the world by the public turned out not to be part of it, such a belief could be judged false. More precisely, there is a distinction between two claims: the minimalist realist position is true; the public believes the minimalist realist position is true. I think that both claims are true. However, I recognize that many reject the first claim. This does not matter. All I need for recognition of the importance of the lack of a scientific foundation for race is agreement that the public thinks the minimalist realist position is true. This is because a commitment to the minimalist realist position is embedded in the general acceptance of science, and the general acceptance of science is embedded in the received opinion about race. Furthermore, if science is accepted as the final authority on physical reality and race is not physically real according to relevant scientific information, then there is a contradiction in both accepting science and believing that race is physically real.

As a realist oneself, or as a student of the realism of others, the best way to determine which putative physical objects exist, and to study them, is via the special methodology of the physical sciences. One general reason for this is the broad goal of science to describe (real or existing) things and relations, without committing logical fallacies. Western science insists that direct observations of objects be replicable and not dependent on unique conditions of observation or unique traits of particular observers. In this way, besides being logical and empirical, the special methodology of science purports to be objective. The duplicable acquisition of scientific information means that science can be shared; the objectivity of science gives it a social dimension.

Insofar as information about a mind-independent physical world can be obtained through sensory perception, with results shared by multiple observers, the objectivity of science is congruent to the objectivity of what realists believe is real. This congruence has a positive or active dimension and a negative or passive one. Some contemporary thinkers appear able to accept the latter without the former. The positive dimension involves new intellectual and technological projects that result from scientific belief in the existence of certain entities, that is, from the ontology of science. This is the dimension in which the technologies associated with modern Western science have already changed both the natural and social worlds and will continue to do so. The negative dimension of the congruence between the ontologies of science and ordinary reality is the cognitive effect of lack of scientific evidence for things otherwise believed to exist. Entities posited in earlier times, such as witches, ghosts, vapors, phlogiston, humors, and so forth, for which science has yielded no evidence of existence, are no longer believed to exist today by educated people. The same can be said for taxonomies such as phrenology and astrology. Many who are skeptical and resistant regarding the positive dimension of scientific ontology easily let go of beliefs in the existence of these now apparently fictitious things. Even contemporary postmodernists who would bracket or dismiss the claims for objectivity and realism in science, because they think that such claims are culturally contingent, do not thereby subscribe to what are now considered superstitions among those who accept the objective and realist claims. The negative ontology of science is more pervasive than the positive, and more easily accepted by its critics.

Finally, an argument could be made that a commitment to even minimal physical realism *should* entail a commitment to accept the conclusions of scientists as true. I won't make that argument here, although I think it is sound (meaning it has true premises from which conclusions are validly deduced). Suffice it to say that the educated public exhibits beliefs and behavior that appear to be based on prior commitments to accept the conclusions of science about physical reality as true. Again, I do not mean to depend on this argument from authority, but am referring to it to be able to assert the following. If educated people believe that scientists believe that something, in this case biological race, exists, and scientists do not believe that the thing exists, then there is a problem for educated belief. The problem can be solved in three ways: (1) Reject the findings of physical science in general; (2) reject the findings of physical science in this particular case; (3) remove biological race from secular ontology. The first option is not feasible. The second option requires making a special case for biological race, which cannot be done without begging the question of whether race has a scientific foundation. The case for the scientific nonexistence of biological race is straightforward and consistent with (accepted) scientific cases for the nonexistence of many other things. The best option is the third: remove biological race from secular ontology. This third option follows rather easily from a philosophical analysis of the contemporary science that is relevant to the existence or nonexistence of biological race. However, because the modern idea of biological race originated in modern biology and spread through application to medicine, social science, common sense, public policy, the arts and liberatory theory, the elimination of the idea of biological race requires thorough criticism of many disciplinary as well as informal subjects and practices. This criticism and elimination would constitute a major paradigm shift in an important area of human life in society.

Philosophy of Biology and Race

I have mainly so far been talking about philosophy of science in general terms, although it should be clear that biology is the specific science yielding information about race. Biology is the study of living things, which are far less stable, regular, and predictable than the subjects of the other physical sciences. Although biologists work under the same general empirical and logical constraints as physicists and chemists, their models of explanation are different because their subjects are less uniform than those in the other sciences. For one example, evolutionary biology is a study of the history of particular species, and its particularity precludes some of the abstraction of classificatory schemes typical in physics or chemistry. Historical explanations may imply lawlike generalizations, but they are always constrained by the fact that their subjects occur but once.

Living individuals and species are distinctive, not merely because they are dynamic systems—dynamic systems exist in the inanimate physical sciences. Living things are distinctive because they are noncyclical, constantly changing systems whose past weakly determines their present (which weakly determines their future). Richard Lewontin explains that the determination or causal connection is weak, because until some events rather than others occur, it cannot be known what outcomes will be. Changes in living things are weakly determined also because multiplicities of causes, which may be genetic, developmental, or environmental, interact in ways that do not yield straightforward inferences about the effects of singular causal factors.[8]

The absence of closed abstract explanatory models in biology does not mean that explanations in biology are not scientific. Rather, biological explanations become tentative beyond the point where methodologies from the physical sciences can be applied to living things and systems. The fact that knowledge claims must become tentative after a certain point fulfills a fundamental empirical ideal of precision about the point where knowledge ceases. Nonetheless, sometimes, at the point where knowledge ceases, it is evident that a quest for further knowledge about a particular subject could be based only on a fundamental misunderstanding of what the subject is. This book should make evident how race lacks the basis in science it was believed to have. And, it should also be further evident that there is no possibility that race, as what was mistakenly believed to have a basis in science, could ever have some other basis in science.

The Stakes

The reader may grant that I can make the case I'm claiming and ask, So what? Since ideas about race are formulated and play out in parts of society far removed from philosophical analysis of science, what could possibly be at stake with such analysis? At stake is the place of biological notions of race in rational secular society. This is not a question of whether "race should be eliminated" toward the realization of a progressive nightmare where racists will continue to discriminate and victims will have no redress because they will no longer be able to identify themselves. Rather, it concerns everyone's comfortable assumption that what they mean by race is something biological. Once the biology of race is put to rest, "race" will look and feel differently to people of all races. What we now accept as race will not have the same motivational force. Will that end racism? Only to the extent that racism is dependent on the assumption that race is biological, which is an empirical matter. My own guess is that racism is highly dependent on biological assumptions. What we do know, independently of the link between ideas of biological race and racism, is that the idea of biological race creates a perceived distance among human beings that is believed to be a natural difference. At the very least, that perception is now at stake, again, for everyone. I will say more about these issues in the last chapter of the book.

1.
Philosophical Racial Essentialism: Hume and Kant

Background

The kinds of oppression and discrimination that are now associated with *racism* have a longer history than the idea of race. Varied forms of clannishness, tribalism, regionalism, and xenophobia can be traced to the earliest days of recorded human history, and there is evidence of group-based conflict and competition among ancient *Homo sapiens*, hominids, and other primates. Chauvinism based on nationality and religion also predate racism and *racialism*, or belief in the existence of races. Much of what is now considered racism instantiates more specific and more general types of discrimination than that directly resulting from biological ideas about race. For instance, people can be described as racist about skin color or ethnicity, which are more specific than race, and about gender or human species identity, which are more general than race.[1] Ideas of race as human biological typology, and the racism(s) distinctively associated with them, did not appear in Western culture, science, or philosophy before the eighteenth century.[2] This is partly because of the historical origins of the modern science of biology and partly because of the historical development of Western colonialism, which was justified by systems of human classification privileging Europeans and (white) Americans.[3]

The Western philosophical contribution to scientific ideas of race is difficult to assess in terms of motive and influence. Were the primary philosophers of race influenced by the external economic and cultural events of colonialism, so that their speculations about hierarchical human taxonomy were mere rationalizations for the injustices committed by Europeans as they expanded into Africa and the Americas? That is, was the primary philosophical thought on race influenced by what we would call external societal pressures? Or, were philosophies of race developed autonomously, based on the best information available in intellectual contexts sheltered from external social and economic forces? And, whether externally influenced or autonomous, was this thought innocent of the kind of malice that today would qualify it as racist? Whatever the answers, the philosophical contribution influenced social, political, and scientific formulations of human difference and became a formidable intellectual obstacle to abolitionism and egalitarianism.

The ways in which Hume and Kant described Africans as inferior to whites have received sharp critical attention recently, because according to contemporary standards, both philosophers were virulent white supremacists. However, little if any analysis has been done on the racialism, or ontology of human races, which underlay Hume and Kant's value judgments about what they thought were racial differences. The aim of this chapter is to pinpoint the gaps in their thinking about an ontology of human races. This requires some prior reflection about essentialism, and I will begin with several historical considerations.

Today, it is derogatory to call a thinker or a concept essentialist, in one or both of two ways: a charge is made that nonexistent essences are being posited; a belief in the existence of essences is alleged to be held as a justification for discrimination against people with an assumed essence. Both forms of the derogation can be imprecise because the concept of essences is complicated. There is no empirical foundation for a concept of essences, outside of the nonbiological physical sciences. Moreover, any contemporary concept of essences in the physical sciences would be different from the historical, metaphysical connotations of the term. The extension of *essentialism*, or a notion of essences, into the biological and social sciences is no longer acceptable to most practitioners, although they may sometimes, perhaps unintentionally, presuppose the validity of essentialism. As a result, the use of racial essentialism in cultural contexts and the criticism of such usage makes it necessary to describe three false levels of belief: beliefs that biological things have essences; beliefs that biological essences underlie human cultural or social typologies and cause cultural or psychological essences; beliefs that members of a culture or society are mistaken about the nature of the biological or cultural and psychological essences that cause its typologies. The third level is the most difficult to address when theoretical and practical liberation has been constructed on the basis of nonexistent essences, of any kind, especially when the essences have been posited as foundations for liberatory identities. Indeed, essentialism in the last sense is still evoked as a basis for group solidarity in established nonwhite cultural ideologies.

In the history of philosophy, Aristotle, from the *Metaphysics*, is usually credited with the first empiricist (in the sense of pertaining to existent physical objects) essentialist analysis that could be applied to living things. Aristotle posited the essence of a thing as something in the thing that made it what it was: "Each thing itself, then, and its essence are one and the same in no merely accidental way.... because to know a thing at least is just to *know* its essence."[4] Elliott Sober explains that Aristotelian essences, as the defining component of *species*, were *constitutive*: The essence of a species or natural kind was believed by Aristotle to be present in each member of the species, and it was what made it a member of that species.[5] Aristotle distinguished between essential properties and accidental properties. The essential properties, or essences of things, could not be changed without changing the kinds of things they were. Accidental properties, and changes in them, did not affect identity in this way.

In addition to their ontological, constitutive role, Aristotle thought that essences, but not accidents, were important to study. The study of essences was the proper subject of science, the content of knowledge. With the beginning of early modern empiricism, there was a general philosophical revolt against the a priori methods of Aristotelian scholasticism as a way of gaining knowledge about existing things. It was thought that the scholastics had spent too much time on definition and not enough on observation. The revolt extended to a rejection of the notion of *real essences* as determinants of what individual things were, in taxonomies of natural kinds. Part of the rejection resulted from the difficulty in imagining how real essences could ever be observed, part from skepticism that scientific knowledge could yield certainty as Aristotle and his followers assumed.[6] John Locke argued in the *Essay Concerning Human Understanding* that we can never know real essences if they are substrata that cause the presence of those defining properties that we can observe. The defining properties of physical things, such as the hardness, malleability, and color of gold, are *nominal essences*, according to Locke. Nominal essences are not in things, as essences, but are chosen by us to be defining (or necessary and sufficient conditions) of classifiable things, based on human interests and systems of meanings.

> This then, in short, is the case: *Nature makes many particular Things, which do agree* one with another, in many sensible Qualities and probably too, in their internal frame and Constitution: but 'tis not this real Essence that distinguishes them into *Species*; 'tis *Men*, who, taking occasion from the Qualities they find united in them, and wherein, they observe often several individuals to agree, *range them into Sorts, in order to their meaning*, for the convenience of comprehensive signs.[7]

Locke did not deny the existence of real essences, but, as Irving Copi notes, he was content to posit them as unobservable causes of nominal essences.[8] It is now widely accepted that what Aristotle called "essences" and Locke called "real essences" have been successfully identified in some physical sciences, such as chemistry.[9] In such sciences, there would seem to be no need for a concept of Lockean nominal essences because any observable real essences would serve as nominal essences as well. However, the situation is different in the biological sciences. Most theorists and researchers do not now believe that biological natural kinds have real essences. In addition, there is debate about whether they have what Locke considered to be nominal essences, or characteristics present in all or most members of a natural kind that it makes sense *to define* as determining membership in that kind. More will be said about methods of biological classification, in future chapters. The point to be taken here for an understanding of racialist essentialism is that in its origins, the eighteenth- and nineteenth-century idea of race was a particular instance of [the ideas of] Aristotelian essences or Lockean real essences. This essentialist modern idea of race was anachronistic in its time, because empiricist philosophers who used it would have had the benefit of Locke's seventeenth-century critique of Aristotelian essences.

It should be emphasized that both Aristotelian and Lockean essentialism pertain to physical reality. When contemporary critics identify something as racialist, essentialist, or racist, they are often talking about presumed links between biological real or nominal essences, on the one side, and psychology and culture on the other side. That is, they are talking about relations. By contrast, Aristotelian essences and Lockean real essences were [supposed to be] actually in physical things. However, neither Aristotle nor Locke seems to have thought that anything resembling biological racial essences were determinant of human psychology or culture. Ivan Hannaford notes that in the *Physiognomonica*, which is commonly attributed to Aristotle, the author rejects as indicative of psychological or cultural difference the kinds of physical traits that later in history came to be associated with racial difference.[10] Locke did not have an idea of biological race as something that could be associated with cultural difference. In his day, politically and morally important human differences were mainly associated with differences in religious belief and affiliation. In his *Letter Concerning Toleration*, he uses an example of what today would resemble racial discrimination to argue for the absurdity of discrimination based on religious difference:

> Suppose this Business of Religion were let alone, and that there were some other Distinction made between men and men, upon account of their different Complexions, Shapes and Features, so that those who have black Hair (for example) or gray Eyes, should not enjoy the same Privileges as other Citizens ... can it be doubted but these Persons, thus distinguished from others by the Colour of their Hair and Eyes, and united together by one common Persecution, would be as dangerous to the Magistrate, as any other that had associated themselves merely upon the account of Religion?[11]

Locke's analogy is a kind of reductio ad absurdum and it underscores how far he was from drawing important human distinctions on the basis of differences in physical appearance. Indeed, in the context of nominal essences in the *Essay* discussion mentioned above, he is at times unsure, given the existence of "monsters," that there are real divisions between human and animal species, apart from where, given the nature of our ideas, it is convenient to draw boundaries.[12] Assuming that for Locke, as for us, differences between humans and animals would always have to be greater than differences within the human group, and assuming that Lockean real essences were, like Aristotelian essences, constitutive, Locke could not have thought there were differences in real essences between human groups.[13] Furthermore, in his discussion of personal identity, also in the *Essay*, Locke notes that shape *seems* to be part of the definition or nominal essence of human beings, because we would deny membership in the category of humanity to cats and parrots which could speak, think, and even philosophize![14] While skin color differences were acknowledged in Locke's day, they were not associated with what would be considered racial difference now or even then. During the early days of the British mercantilism, the Crown encouraged slave trading as a way to develop a monopoly over the transportation of British goods. Sea merchants were resistant at first. In 1621, Richard Jobson refused to accept as commodities, "any who had our own shape."[15] That is, Jobson, like Locke after him in the cat and parrot examples in the *Essay*, thought that sameness in physical shape was sufficient for sameness in species identity, and along with that, sameness in being worthy of moral consideration.

The notion that physical biology alone *determines* culture and psychology does not have a long history in the concept of race, because it has only been since the 1930s that theorists in the human biological sciences have broadly agreed that cultural differences among human groups are not inherited along with [what are believed to be] physical racial differences.[16] Indeed, only after culture had been distinguished from hereditary biology did it become possible to debate the extent to which biology did or did not cause the cultural differences associated with distinct biological races. Before the conceptual separation of culture from biology, racialist essentialists generally assumed that culture and psychology were inherited *within* distinct biological racial groups, presumably via the Aristotelian or real essences of race. Such mythology is evident not only in Hume and Kant's speculations about race, but in writings by political theorists such as Thomas Jefferson, as well as in the widely accepted pronouncements of white supremacist cultural authorities, during the late nineteenth and early twentieth centuries. However, neither Hume nor Kant made explicit political or social proposals about race. Their writing on race was ostensibly about the ontology and taxonomy of race: It provided a philosophical foundation for subsequent anthropometric studies of racial difference, as well as for white supremacist political doctrine. The philosophy of science question that needs to be answered for each of them is, Where and to what extent did they go beyond the evidence available to them and the logic they otherwise followed?

Hume on Race

Hume's views on human racial difference occur in a footnote within "Of National Characters," first published in the 1754 edition of his *Essays Moral, Political and Literary*.[17] Richard Popkin's account of the broader intellectual context of this footnote leaves little doubt that Hume was aware of the importance of the footnote's content, because he wrote it during a public debate about whether the human species had one origin or several that corresponded to different races. Hume disagreed with Compte de Buffon's *monogenic* environmental account of human difference, which was based on earlier writings by Montesquieu. The monogenic racial theorists attempted to explain how differences in climate, living conditions, and diet could have caused apparent differences in human groups, and they concluded that these group differences were neither inherent nor permanent. In contrast, the *polygenic* theory of distinct origins for different races was used to argue that Africans, Asians, and Indians were permanently inferior to whites.[18] That is, both the monogenicists and polygenicists began with the premise of white superiority, but differed about its nature.

Hume's discussion in "On National Characters" begins with a caution against the vulgar tendency to make sweeping generalizations about group traits. He insists that the causes of national characters are *moral*, that is, psychological and cultural, as opposed to physical. He rejects the environmentalist thesis on the grounds that human beings develop their cultures and characters through imitation caused by continued, close social interaction. Hume believes that these moral causes operate on people individually, and that the effects of different types of government are in principle no different from the effects of different professional conditions, such as those of soldiers and priests.

Hume claims empirical support for the thesis that cultural differences have cultural causes: "If we run over the globe, or revolve the annals of history, we shall discover every where signs of a sympathy or contagion of manners, none of the influence of air or climate."[19] He adduces several groups of facts for this thesis: long-established governments are accompanied by stable national characters; the borders of contiguous small nations mark differences in national characters; changes in national character accompany changes in national boundaries that have been drawn as the result of historical events, independently of air or climate; people who leave their nations of origin maintain their manners if they continue to associate with fellow countrymen; national characters change over history; there is a blending of national characters among neighbors; some nations, such as England, have mixed characters within them because they have diverse groups of citizens. Hume insists that even in the polar regions and tropics, extremes of temperature do not directly influence national characters, although they may create social conditions that do. He observes that the characters of nations vary within temperate climates and notes that it is difficult to generalize about people farthest north or south in these climates.[20]

It is at this point in the discussion that the infamous footnote occurs. The footnote became infamous because of the use made of it later. But even in the development of Hume's text it is jarring, because before it appears, Hume's subject seems to be all of humanity. His theory of social and psychological causes for national differences implies that human beings merit a more elevated model of analysis than the merely biological taxonomy used by Buffon. However, the footnote makes it clear that his subject is not all of humanity, but only white Europeans, and the basis for his taxonomy of human beings may not be nation, culture, religion, or even race, but *species*. This species basis for division is evident in the following footnote passage:

> I am apt to suspect the negroes and in general all the other species of men (for there are four or five different kinds) to be naturally inferior to the whites. There never was a civilized nation of any other complexion than white, nor even any individual eminent either in action or speculation. No ingenious manufactures amongst them, no arts, no sciences. On the other hand, the most rude and barbarous of the whites, such as the ancient Germans, the present Tartars, have still something eminent about them, in their valour, form of government, or some other particular. Such a uniform and constant difference could not happen, in so many countries and ages, if nature had not made an original distinction betwixt these breeds of men. Not to mention our colonies, there are Negroe slaves dispersed all over Europe, of which none ever discovered any symptoms of ingenuity; tho' low people, without education, will start up amongst us, and distinguish themselves in every profession. In Jamaica indeed they talk of one negroe as a man of parts and learning; but 'tis likely he is admired for very slender accomplishments, like a parrot, who speaks a few words plainly.[21]

Richard Popkin refers to Hume's sweeping generalization about Negro intellectual inferiority as "Hume's racial law," and indeed it was invoked in subsequent arguments from authority in the contexts of both racist and antiracist discourse.[22] It is not evident, however, what this "law" is about, because Hume does not clearly distinguish between races and species. Possibly, Hume did mean to address the subject of racial differences among human beings and used the term 'species' to mean the same thing as 'race.' But, his use of 'species' could also be taken literally to mean that the non-white "breeds of men" were so different from the white breed that the same principles could not be used to account for their cultural development. This is odd because in his essay "Of the Populousness of Ancient Peoples," which was written before 1750, he claims that civilization rises and falls at different times among different nations and that it is difficult to identify either superior historical periods or superior nations:

> Stature and force of body, length of life, even courage and extent of genius, seem hitherto to have been naturally, in all ages, pretty much the same. The arts and sciences, indeed, have flourished in one period, and have decayed in another. . . . As far, therefore, as observation reaches, there is no universal difference discernible in the human species.[23]

If Hume meant to talk about race in the footnote in "Of National Characters," one would expect him to have justified the basis for racial divisions, because he has earlier said that climate and other environmental factors having physical effects, such as skin color (which was widely held to be a racial trait by the time he wrote), are not sufficient to account for the important differences in national characters. He accepts an environmentalist explanation for physical differences, but not for cultural ones that are the result of custom and association. Nonetheless, the footnote does not extend the custom-and-association account of difference to a comparison of nonwhites with whites, or comparisons between nonwhite groups. Therefore, Hume must have thought that something other than custom and association caused the differences between whites and nonwhites. If custom and association could influence the culture and intellectual achievement of nonwhites, as it did whites, then Hume would have had to allow that the cultures of nonwhites, like the cultures of whites, were subject to change and development. Hume did not allow for this possibility, because he posited the differences between whites and nonwhites as fundamental and permanent. But again, if he did mean to talk about the difference between whites and nonwhites as a racial difference, he has not told us wherein he thought that difference lay or what its nature was. It cannot be something physical, because physical things do not cause differences in psychology and culture, and it cannot be cultural or associational, because those factors would allow for nonwhites to develop as whites do.

If Hume meant to talk about species, and not race, in the infamous footnote, then one would expect him to provide some independent cause, other than the cultural difference that needs to be explained, as the basis for the division of whites and nonwhites into four or five different species. Indeed, early in the same essay he asserts: "It is a maxim in all philosophy, that causes which do not appear are to be taken as not existing."[24] Hume might have accepted the prevailing taxonomy of race, and thought that a species difference caused it. But then, he would have had to define 'species' and explain how or in what way whites and nonwhites belonged to different ones and how this caused the racial differences he believed evident.

Something like real essences would seem to be necessary to account for the kinds of differences that Hume implies accompany human races or species. He makes no suggestion of cultural relativity, bias among observers, or reliance on convention in dividing human groups into the white and nonwhite ones, any or all of which variables would allow for a Lockean notion of nominal essences in delineating human taxonomy. At the time Hume wrote, no one had an adequate account of the natural causes of species and the divisions among them, but then, as now, it was popularly assumed that differences in species, especially those dividing humans from other animals, were important and (practically) impossible to change. Scientific descriptions of racial differences and the theories behind racial taxonomies did not exist when Hume wrote. His generalization about Negro inferiority is backed up with a polygenic assumption that seems informative only if it is assumed that something about each of the human groups, existing in all members in a constitutive way, determines it to be the group it is. And of course, once such an assumption is disclosed, it must be justified or rejected. As an empiricist philosopher, Hume could not have justified a notion of real essences as constitutive of different races. But, he does not examine his easy assumption that races exist, or consider that the racial differences posited by him would have to be necessary, rather than contingent.

In 1770, James Beattie objected to the obvious lack of empirical proof for Hume's generalization, on several unexceptional grounds: Europeans had themselves been uncivilized two thousand years earlier; the civilizations of all Negroes were unknown to Hume; there were many counterexamples to Hume's claims of Negro inferiority.[25] For the 1776 edition of the volume in which "Of National Characters" appeared, Hume changed the first passage below, to the second one:

(1) I am apt to suspect the negroes and in general all other species of men (for there are four or five different kinds) to be naturally inferior to the whites. There never was a civilized nation of any other complexion than white. . . .

(2) I am apt to suspect the negroes to be naturally inferior to the whites. There scarcely ever was a civilized nation of that complexion, not even of individual eminent in action or speculation. . . .[26]

The second version of Hume's generalization places the burden of proof on the term 'natural' in a way that opens the door for what was later to develop into combined physical and psychological theories of racial difference. Here, without spelling out a polygenic racial or species hypothesis, Hume links intellectual achievement with skin shade (complexion) as a statistical observation. There is empirical restraint in this formulation. Still, having forgone the constant conjunction of dark skin shade and cultural inferiority, and having ruled out environmental causes of culture, Hume has no basis for a causal connection between skin shade and culture (in either direction) and no evidence for the existence of a third factor that could cause both skin shade and culture. He may have been speaking idly and simply not bothered to think through the conceptual problems. This negligence would be pointed, given his contemporary debate between monogenicists and polygenicists. It is as though Hume did not think the question important and was prepared to decide it on the basis of unexamined popular prejudice, except that Hume himself was a major element in such prejudice. A more favorable interpretation is that Hume thought he was merely describing a phenomenon that others would someday explain. But, in that case, it is uncharacteristic of him to accept a future discovery of the cause of racial difference as a reason for accepting that difference. Why not stick to his own maxim, "causes which do not appear are to be taken as nonexisting"?

Kant on Race

If Hume's discussion of race is superficial, Kant's is too deep. Kant had a biological theory of race that partially anticipated evolutionary theories of species. He also had a theory of hereditary national characters, which could be used to conflate biological race and culture, or posit a third factor as a cause of both biological racial traits and the cultural differences associated with them. Kant was a monogenicist, because he accepted Buffon's rule that the criterion for same species membership was the ability to produce fertile offspring. But, he rejected similarity as a foundation for biological taxonomy, because it did not go beyond mere "academic" classification. Kant sought a "natural system for the comprehension" based on genealogy, or heredity. He reasoned that humans must all descend from the same *stem*. This meant that humans are members of the same family, because to hypothesize different origins of descent for dissimilar groups within the same species would needlessly multiply entities.[27] Kant was correct about monogenicism, but for a mistaken reason and an empirically inadequate reason. The mistaken reason was Buffon's rule, because it is possible for different species to interbreed. Human groups all belong to the same species because there is *intergrading* between groups, or gradual, continuous variation in traits that distinguish groups, as well as independent genetic evidence of recent common descent.[28] Kant's empirically inadequate reason for monogenicism was the principle of economy, the empirically adequate reason being subsequent evidence of common descent. Or rather, if economy or simplicity is accepted as a theoretical standard, the empirical rationale for it would be that simple hypotheses are easier to test and falsify.[29]

Kant anticipated Darwin in his initial insistence that an explanation of biological difference was necessary and that such an explanation would involve heredity. Kant's theory of differences within species made full use of this genealogical criterion:

> Among the deviations—i.e., the hereditary differences of animals belonging to a single stock—those which, when transplanted (displaced to other areas), maintain themselves over protracted generation, and which also generate hybrid young whenever they interbreed with other deviations of the same stock, are called *races*. Those which at every transplantation maintain the distinctiveness of their deviation and so preserve their resemblance, yet when interbreeding with others do not necessarily generate hybrids, are called *sports*; but those which maintain resemblance often and persistently are called *varieties*. Conversely, the deviation which

generates hybrids with others, yet which after being transplanted grad-
ually disappears, is called a special *strain*.[30]

Thus, within species, Kant sets up a taxonomy of race and hybrid. Sports
are false races because they do not generate hybrids; and strains are also false
races because they are the effects of environmental factors. It is not clear
exactly how Kant defines varieties, as distinct from sports, because they are
permanently hereditary and presumably do not generate hybrids since only
races do that. His examples of varieties are illuminating in a way that he
clearly did not intend, as I will explain after discussion of the conceptual
problems with his notions of race and hybridity. In the paragraph following
the passage quoted above, Kant applies his taxonomy of races, hybrids, and
sports to Negroes and whites:

> In this way Negroes and whites are not different species of humans (for
> they belong presumably to one stock), but they are different races, for
> each perpetuates itself in every area, and they generate between them
> children that are necessarily hybrid, or blendings (mulattoes). On the
> other hand, blonds or brunettes are not different races of whites, for a
> blond man can also get from a brunette woman altogether blond chil-
> dren, even though each of these deviations maintains itself throughout
> protracted generations under any and all transplantations. Hence, some-
> times whites generate sports.[31]

It is obvious, but nonetheless worth emphasizing, that a philosophical or
theoretical belief in race is necessarily a belief that there are at least two races.
Kant made use of this implication. If the two passages quoted from "On the
Different Races of Man" are combined, Kant may be interpreted as defining
race in this way:

> [K] Two different groups with the same ancestry are distinct races, if and
> only if, each group has distinct hereditary traits and members of the two
> groups generate hybrid young when they interbreed.

Notice that there are no criteria for racial membership or for the kind of distinctive traits that are candidates for producing hybridity. We are not told
whether the whole individual offspring is a hybrid, or merely the trait that
is a blended or hybrid trait. If the whole individual is a hybrid, then something general must determine racial membership. If only the blendable trait
is a hybrid, then it must constitute the racial identity of the whole offspring.
That is, either the whole causes the blendable trait, or the blendable trait
causes the whole. Something like an Aristotelian or Lockean real essence
would have to be at work as a general or specific, necessary and sufficient
cause of race. Kant tells us that Negroes and whites are different races

because they have hereditary differences and their interbreeding produces hybrids. Here, a problem of the criterion for difference, or in Kant's language, *deviation*, arises. How do we know what kinds of things count as the hereditary differences that demarcate races? The absence of an empirical answer to this question reduces Kant's definition of race to this:

> [K'] Two different groups with the same ancestry are distinct races, if and only if, each group has distinct hereditary traits and members of the two groups generate mixed race young when they interbreed.

K' looks circular if the meaning of 'race' is no different in cases of pure race and mixed race. Although Kant seems to place an extra definitional burden on 'mixed race,' he offers no clues about what this burden is or why it is placed there. As a result, K' is an interesting inversion of the main problem considered in present discussions of mixed race. Theorists who debate the desirability of mixed race identity do not now assume that there is a different meaning of 'race' in cases of pure and mixed race, and they base realism about mixed race on realism about race:[32] If race is real, then so is mixed race; if race is unreal, then so is mixed race. Kant bases realism about race on realism about mixed race, but, again, his reasons are mysterious.

Kant assumes that both blonds and brunettes are whites (which makes one wonder how he would describe the hair color of nonwhites), and he concludes that they are not races because their offspring do not [ever?] have blended hair color. We can see here that his unstated criterion for racial difference between Negroes and whites depends on the assumed blending of skin color in offspring who have both Negro and white parents. For Kant, it seems to be skin color that has the Aristotelian, or Lockean, real essentializing property or properties that determines racial identity. If Kant had based racial difference on height, hair color, or eye color, instead of skin color, or if he had observed, or allowed for the observation of, apparent blending in hereditary traits other than skin color, or if he had known of cases where skin color did not blend with "interbreeding," he might not have concluded that Negroes and whites were different races. But, this speculation is anachronistic and naive. It is anachronistic because Kant did not know, as Mendel and his twentieth-century heirs were to discover, that the traits of human physical variety, including those designated as racial, are inherited independently of one another. He therefore could not have known that what he (and others to this day) term "skin color" is probably a phenotypical effect of a number of genes that vary independently (*probably*, because all of the genes associated with skin color have not yet been identified and the precise development of skin color phenotypes is not understood).[33] Kant also did not know that a concept of blending can be applied neither to the heredity of entire organisms nor to individual genes, because hereditary traits are passed on via individual genes, and individual genes are discrete entities that neither mix nor blend with other genes. But even had the facts about skin color and blending been as he assumed, there is no biological basis on which to decide that the presence, absence, or blending of the single hereditary trait he picked out is sufficient to characterize entire organisms in biological typology. (It is ironic that apparent blending of skin color in children whose parents have evident differences in that trait is today used as a reason to reject established racial divisions.)

It is naive to speculate that Kant would not have classified races as he did, given more information about human heredity, because he never questions that Negroes and whites (or, at least Negroes and whites—the same could be said for any other two races in his taxonomy) are two distinct races. After laying out his species-race-hybrid typology, he describes white groups and the "Hindustanic" and "Kalmuck" races. He then simply asserts, "The reason for assuming the Negroes and Whites to be fundamental races is self-evident."[34]

This assumption aside, let us now return to Kant's examples of varieties, the second type of deviation after sports, "those which maintain resemblances often and persistently":

> Whatever pertains to varieties and, therefore is in itself hereditary (although not by that token persistent), can nonetheless bring forth in time, by means of matings that remain within the same families, what I call the *family strain*, where something characteristic becomes so deeply rooted in the generative force that it comes near to being a sport and perpetuates itself as does the latter. This is supposed to have been observed in the old nobility of Venice, especially among the women. At least, in the newly discovered island of Tahiti the noblewomen are on the whole taller than the commoners. It was the opinion of de Maupertuis that it would be possible to produce a naturally noble strain of humans anywhere, in which intellect, competence, and integrity would be hereditary, based upon the formation of a family strain rendered permanent through careful selection of the deviant births from out of the conformant births.[35]

Without positing the existence of races, it would still be possible to recognize what Kant is here calling varieties. His notion of humanly selected breeding anticipates Darwin's idea of sexual selection, as well as the broader evolutionary concept of reproductive success. It also anticipates nineteenth-century eugenics. As well, there is a contemporary view that the formation of what are believed to be distinct racial groups is the result of cultural sanctions such as antimiscegenation laws and racial segregation in the past, and prevailing preferences for mates of the same race.[36] Had Kant not assumed the existence of distinct human races, he could have derived the biological differences he wanted to account for, from his concept of variety. To be sure, he goes on to assume that intellectual and moral virtues are, or could be, hereditary (an assumption shared by nineteenth-century eugenicists). He further assumes, filling in the gap left by Hume, that there is a general hereditary factor, that is, the *generative force*, which accounts for both human biology and culture. I will now bring this chapter to a close by considering that aspect of Kant's racial essentialism.

Kant may have essentialized skin color as a perceptible criterion for racial difference, but he knew that something weightier than skin color would have to be at work in order to sustain the kinds of differences implied by racial taxonomy. For Kant, racial taxonomy in the biological sense was external to human psychic life, a part of natural history or what he called *geography*. He believed that the laws of human culture, morality, and psychology were to be found in the study of what he called *anthropology*.[37] The possibility of human self-improvement was the motivation for Kant's cultural analyses in *Anthropology from a Pragmatic Point of View*, because "pragmatic knowledge of man aims at what man makes, can, or should make of himself as a freely acting being."[38] Kant held that the inner nature or character of man is his distinctively human essence that makes it possible for him to develop as a civilized being. He believed that character varies among nations, however, because *talent* is not evenly distributed among human groups. And he concluded that the only race capable of progress in the arts and sciences is white Europeans: "The white race possesses *all* motivating forces and talents *in itself*."[39]

In a manner similar to Hume, Kant restricted his account of developments in civilization to white groups, effectively writing nonwhites out of history. Kant speculated that differences in national characters were the results of unseen formative causes and geographical differences, which were evident in "the distinctive feeling of the beautiful and the sublime." He drew subtle distinctions among the inhabitants of France, Spain, England, and Germany (who were superior to all). But, when it came to Africans, his taxonomy did not branch into nations, and he switched from the anthropological subject of national characters to the geographical subject of race, taking a short step back to Hume:

> The Negroes of Africa have by nature no feeling that rises above the *trifling*. Mr. Hume challenges anyone to cite a single example in which a Negro has shown talents, and asserts that among the hundreds of thousands of blacks who are transported elsewhere from their countries, although many of them have even been set free, still not a single one was ever found who presented anything great in art or science or any other praise-worthy quality, even though among the whites some continually rise aloft from the lowest rabble, and through superior gifts earn respect in the world. So fundamental is the difference between these two races of man, and it appears to be as great in regard to mental capacities as in color.[40]

Elsewhere, in an aside reminiscent of Hume's footnote, Kant wrote, "this fellow was quite black from head to foot, a clear proof that what he said was stupid."[41] Still, he was not making the superficially bigoted claim that black skin is accompanied by stupidity, as Hume may have done. Rather, Kant seemed to believe that intelligence and skin color were inextricably and probably necessarily connected to distinctive real essences of race, that is, the unseen "formative causes." That was the basis on which he assumed that darkness of hereditary skin shade was inversely proportional to level of intelligence, as well as to moral virtues and their development.

Returning to the different kinds of cultural and philosophical essentialism discussed earlier, we can see that Kant employed them all, except for Lockean nominalism. He believed in Aristotelian constitutive essences for racial groups and thought that such essences were the likely subject of science. This meant that he thought he had knowledge of what Locke would have called real essences of race. To say that Kant stereotyped nonwhites is an understatement, because he assumed that racial essences existed as permanent links between biology and culture. The way Kant wrote nonwhites out of history also made it possible to exclude them from the realm of moral humanity. History, for Kant and other Enlightenment thinkers, was a teleological process in which the human race, as a species, could perfect itself morally, in no small part through the acquisition of knowledge, especially scientific knowledge.[42] Historical development was civilization, and a people's knowledge of its history was its culture. To borrow K. Anthony Appiah's terminology, Hume was an *extrinsic* racist because, given his empiricism, he would have had to say that the connection between biological race and intelligence was contingent, whereas Kant was an *intrinsic* racist insofar as there was nothing in his other philosophical commitments to restrain him from asserting that the connection was necessary.[43]

Most educated people today, and certainly those in public positions, would reject Hume and Kant's racism and white supremacy out of hand. Most biologists would, in addition, not credit an assumption that races exist, without careful empirical consideration. However, Hume and Kant's kind of unquestioning belief in the existence of human biological races lingers to this day in private folk belief and in many quasi-empirical and "soft" intellectual areas, which include: defenses of anthropological typologies and critiques of these typologies, which do no more than question their hierarchical structure; claims of race-based links in the heritability of intelligence; a refusal in both public health and social science to take seriously the ultimate nonbiological causes of pathologies linked to race; essentialist assumptions in much of the scholarship and activism of race-based identity politics; race-based pride, hate, and shame, as well as unexamined racial identities. In the next two chapters, current scientific information that is relevant to the existence of race will be considered. Subsequent chapters will address some of these "softer" areas. We will see that in saying race is unreal, many thinkers seem not to understand how and why *physical* race is unreal. Instead, they content themselves with understanding why racism or white supremacy is unjustified. Combating racism and white supremacy is indeed a moral and political issue of the highest priority. But, the crucial scientific issue concerning race is the lack of a biological, empirical foundation for the social taxonomies of human race that are based on the assumption that the scientific foundation exists. Against Kant, to state the obvious, there is no evidence in the biological sciences for the existence of any one human physical trait that constitutively determines membership in a human race or subspecies. Kantian racial essences are thus *metaphysical* and empirically impossible. For Kant, racial essences serve a general function of human biological and hereditary identity, and they cause the particular traits he associated with race, namely skin color and the varied psychic "talents." It is the nonexistence of racial essences in this general physical sense, for any of the so-called human races, which has to be recognized in order to understand real human biological variety.

2.

Geography and Ideas of Race

Race Factors

Ever since the early nineteenth century, when the idea of race as biological human difference became effective for the organization of society, the public has been confident that evident human differences in skin color and morphology could be explained by descriptions of general race factors knowable to scientists. For example, it is believed that black people have some physical thing that makes them black and causes dark skin shades. General race factors, such as blackness, are believed to determine racial membership and cause specific racial traits.

The public has never explicitly required that general race factors be observable to it, but is usually satisfied if the specific race traits are observable. For instance, it is supposed that anyone can see that a black person has "dark" skin. The public will even accept racial identities at odds with observable physical traits, for instance fair-skinned blacks and dark-skinned whites. Still, in the jumble of everyday life, average people sort others into races based on their appearances, without questioning the existence of general race factors, or separating the assumption of their existence from the process of racial sorting. The public does not have theories about its epistemology or ontology concerning what it thinks is race, and it doesn't seem to need them, either. In ordinary experience, the biological taxonomy of race appears simply to be given in hereditary human differences that are evident "on the street." Anyone who denies the reality of race is taken to be denying common evidence of biological variety, which is absurd to do. Not surprisingly, the main business of race concerns the different attitudes and behavior that are attached to differences in appearance assumed to be racial. This is the primary sense in which "race matters" in daily life. That human biological variation in itself does not prove the existence of race is a fact that barely registers. A denial of the existence of biological variation would entail a denial of the existence of biological race. But, biological denial of the existence of race does not entail denial of the existence of biological variation.[1]

The epistemology of race is the process of sorting people into different races, and the criteria for racial membership or identity. The ontology of race rests on evidence for the existence of two or more races, evidence for racial taxonomy in the first place, and its basic premise is either, Yes, there are human races, or, No, there are not human races. We saw in chapter 1 that Hume and Kant simply assumed that there are human races. Ashley Montagu and other mid-twentieth century anthropologists pointed out that any racial taxonomy would require factual support before it was constructed *as a scientific taxonomy*, and the factual support would have to be of a scientific nature and not just ordinary beliefs that there are human races. Such support did not exist when Hume and Kant wrote or when Montagu objected to continued assumptions about it.[2] The empirical scientific support for human racial taxonomy is still not in evidence, and it is important to understand precisely what facts are lacking and where the conceptual gaps occur in the thinking of those who believe that there is now scientific evidence for human racial taxonomy.

Scientists usually prefer to posit observed, rather than unobserved, explanatory entities. But, if there is evidence that a cause, X, exists, a present technological inability to observe X need not mar its empirical respectability. Viruses and genes are examples of explanatory entities that were accepted before they could be directly observed. Atoms and subatomic particles may never be directly observed and may in principle be impossible to ever observe. Therefore, if there were evidence for the existence of general race factors, the fact that they had not, or could not, be directly observed would not necessarily impugn their scientific status. If there were no evidence for general race factors, statistically reliable specific factors might serve as a scientific foundation for the human group differences that the public believes are racial, if there were independent evidence for their existence. Statistically reliable specific race factors would be a weaker scientific foundation for common sense racial taxonomy than general race factors, but they might be useful. For instance, there might be specific biological traits that were present only in all, or even most, people who were socially identified as black, and descriptions of those traits could be used as a biological foundation for definitions of blackness. Knowledge of specific racial factors would be useful beyond definitive purposes, if they were known to be connected with other human traits distinctive to socially identified racial groups. Generally speaking, this kind of connection is the minimum of what the educated public often assumes, is, or someday will be, the result of scientific inquiries about race.

Leaving aside racial essences, which could not be empirical entities, there have been four bases for ideas of physical race in common sense: geographical origins of ancestors; phenotypes or physical appearance of individuals; hereditary traits of individuals; genealogy. Ever since race became a subject in human biology and anthropology, the scientific search for general as well as statistically reliable specific race factors has focused on these four bases in varied combinations. Eighteenth- and nineteenth-century white supremacist scientists claimed that Europeans were culturally and intellectually superior to Africans and Asians, as well as healthier and more beautiful physically.[3] During the nineteenth century, most scientists assumed that human races existed and that each race was distinguished by hereditary factors that determined physical appearance, as well as culture and psychology. Quantitative attempts to measure physical racial differences proceeded from assumptions that scientists could distinguish among members of the different races, based on their appearance and geographical origins, before they made their measurements. As Stephen Jay Gould and others have shown, these assumptions of prescientific difference privileged whites before the anthropometry of cranial capacity (believed to indicate brain size, which indicated intelligence) and limb proportion was undertaken. The actual measurements were then interpreted in ways that supported presumptions of white supremacy, and the raw data was also recorded inaccurately and at times falsified, to corroborate the presumptions.[4]

In the early twentieth century, cross-cultural anthropological studies made it evident that cultural and psychological racial distinctions were the result of historical events and contingencies only, so that they could not be inherited along with the physical traits that were still taken to indicate racial identity.[5] This put the scientific burden of biological racial difference on physical biology alone. Developments in neo-Mendelian heredity theory, human genetics, and evolutionary theory opened the question of whether there were human races in even a restricted physical biological sense. However, assumptions that geographical ancestral origin is an empirical basis for racial difference and identity continue to be held today by humanistic and scientific theorists of race and by the lay public. In this chapter, I will examine the geographical basis of ideas of race, in history and contemporary science.

The History of Geography as a Basis of Race

Most contemporary theorists of race, and critics of racialism and racism, recognize that the modern Western idea of race was constructed, at least in part, as a justification for the unjust treatment of victims of slavery, colonialism, and genocide, in an age when Enlightenment principles required universal justice and equality. The seventeenth-century rights of political subjects, the eighteenth-century rights of men, and the nineteenth- and early-twentieth century democratic notions of individual rights were meant to be restricted to white males, preferably property owners. The rationalization of oppression and unequal treatment of women and nonwhites, compared to white males, has come to be understood as an application of crudely drawn abstract biological taxonomies that favored white males. (Indeed the liberatory scholarship and activism of the last third of the twentieth century developed from that historical thesis.) But within the liberatory tradition, sometimes insufficient attention has been paid to the original and ongoing material conditions of oppression. Geography, as a fact in the world that was a parameter of original oppression, and as an idea later connected to falsely essentialist abstract biological taxonomies, is a crucial material condition in this neglected sense. We saw in chapter 1 that Kant called the entire science of human biological history, "Geography," and that he listed known races according to their geographical points of origin.

Nonwhite racial categories were imposed on people who lived in or came from particular places. Those places—Africa, Asia, America—and the conditions of their discovery by Europeans were conceptualized before biological racial categories were constructed, so that ideas about the places grounded the later taxonomies of biological race. The first modern European attempts to classify and describe non-European groups were made by travelers and traders during the "Age of Discovery." Notions of place preceded even prototypical notions of race. We can assimilate the tones of shock, wonder, and titillation in descriptions of newly discovered non-European places, to later racisms that accompanied later ideas of race, but it is anachronistic to do so. Consider how Amerigo Vespucci's 1503 *Mundus Novis* (Letter on the New World) so captured the imagination of Europeans that the continent likely to have been named for Columbus was called "America." Amerigo described human inhabitants of that continent, not as instances of an abstract classificatory category, but as the denizens of the geographical place that was his main interest:

> Part of this new continent lies in the torrid zone beyond the equator toward the Antarctic pole, for it begins eight degrees beyond the equator. We sailed along this coast until we passed the tropic of Capricorn and found the Antarctic pole fifty degrees higher than the horizon. We advanced to within seventeen and a half degrees of the Antarctic circle, and what I there have seen and learned concerning the nature of those races, their manners, their tractability and the fertility of the soil, the salubrity of the climate, the position of the heavenly bodies in the sky, and especially concerning the fixed stars of the eighth sphere, never seen or studied by our ancestors, these things I shall relate in order.[6]

By 1748, when Georges-Louis Leclerc, Comte de Buffon, wrote *A Natural History, General and Particular*, he was able to catalogue differences in races to correspond with differences in geography, so as to suggest a research program. Buffon's use of geographical differences to explain racial differences was undertaken as a defense of his monogenicism, and that is how it is usually interpreted. But, his assumed close causal connection between geography and race deserves attention in its own right, because it was to become so widespread. Buffon believed not only that continental geographic differences accounted for differences among the major races, but he attempted to relate differences within continents, to differences within individual races:

Africa is not less singular for the uniformity in the figure and colour of its inhabitants, than Africa is remarkable for the variety of men it contains. This part of the world is very ancient, and very populous. The climate is extremely hot; and yet the temperature of the air differs widely in different nations. Their manners also are not less various, as appears from the description I have given of them. All these causes have concurred in producing a greater variety of men in this quarter of the globe than in any other.[7]

After Buffon, Johann Friedrich Blumenbach began his version of monogenicism with the speculation that the primary human race was white. Blumenbach then accounted for the existence of nonwhites with a theory of the ways in which white subgroups had *degenerated* as a result of different geographical conditions. Like Buffon, Blumenbach catalogued races on a geographical basis, but he speculated that geographical factors were the causes of specific racial degenerations. Blumenbach's first two maxims or "corollaries" to his theory of degeneration make this clear: In the first maxim, he posits geographical variations over time as causes of complex human development, in general:

(1) The more causes of degeneration which act in conjunction and the longer they act upon the same species of animals, the more palpably that species may fall off from its primeval conformation. Now no animal can be compared to man in this respect, for he is omnivorous, and dwells in every climate, and is far more domesticated and far more advanced from his first beginnings than any other animal; and so on him the united force of climate, diet, and mode of life must have acted for a very long time.

Blumenbach's second maxim posits geographical variation as a cause of variations within geographically defined human groups, or races.

(2) On the other hand an otherwise sufficiently powerful cause of degeneration may be changed and debilitated by the accession of other conditions, especially if they are as it were opposed to it. Hence everywhere in various regions of the terraqueous globe, even those which lie in the same geographical latitude, still a very different temperature of the air and equally different and generally a contrary effect on the condition of animals may be observed, according as they differ in the circumstances of a higher or lower position, proximity to the sea, or marshes or mountains, or woods, or of a cloudy or serene sky, or some peculiar character of soil, or other circumstances of that kind.[8]

The important difference between Buffon, writing in 1748, and Blumenbach, writing in 1776, is that Blumenbach, with his notion of degeneration, attached a scale of human worth to geographical difference. By the time we get to Hegel, writing in the 1820s, the influence of geography in the formation of races is so great that the full flower of civilization could have been possible only in Europe. Hegel takes European superiority for granted and looks for a geographical explanation in comparing Asians with Europeans.

> Since no one particular type of environment predominates in Europe as it does in the other continents, man too is more universal in character. Those particular ways of life which are tied to different physical contexts do not assume such distinct and peculiar forms as they do in Asia, on whose history they have had so great an effect; for the geographical differences within Europe are not sharply defined. Natural life is also the realm of contingency, however, and only in its universal attributes does it exercise a determining influence commensurate with the principle of the spirit. The character of the Greek spirit, for example, grew out of the soil of Greece, a coastal territory which encourages individual autonomy. Similarly, the Roman Empire could not have arisen in the heart of the continent. Man can exist in all climates; but the climates are of a limited character, so that the power they exercise is the external counterpart to man's inner nature. Consequently, European man also appears naturally freer than the inhabitants of other continents, because no one natural principle is dominant in Europe. Those distinct ways of life which appear in Asia in a state of mutual conflict appear in Europe rather as separate social classes within the concrete state.... The sea provides that wholly peculiar outlet which Asiatic life lacks, the outlet which enables life to step beyond itself. It is this which has invested European political life with the principle of individual freedom.[9]

Thus, for Hegel, geography is not merely a cause of physical difference as it was for Buffon, or of physical and moral difference as it was for Blumenbach, but, in the (convenient) language of other parts of his philosophy, an expression of *spirit*, of which, in the case of race, physical and moral difference is the co-expression. Also, for Hegel, Asia is the only contender to Europe, because he has already removed Africa from the self-aware progression of human history, again based on geography (as that co-expression, with physical and moral difference, of spirit):

> *Africa Proper* is the characteristic part of the whole continent as such. We have chosen to examine this continent first, because it can well be taken as antecedent to our main enquiry. It has no historical interest of its own, for we find its inhabitants living in barbarism and slavery in a land which has not furnished them with any integral ingredient of culture. From the earliest historical times, Africa has remained cut off from all contacts with the rest of the word; it is the land of gold, forever pressing in upon

itself, and the land of childhood, removed from the light of self-conscious history and wrapped in the dark mantle of night. Its isolation is not just a result of its tropical nature, but an essential consequence of its geographical character.[10]

Geography as a Basis of Race in Contemporary Science

Early scientific accounts of the geographical history of *Homo sapiens* were connected with core hypotheses about whether apparent racial differences are the evolutionary effect of migrations from one original location, or the result of different geographical origins for different races. In the eighteenth and nineteenth centuries, *polygenicists* argued that distinct human racial groups had different ancestral geographical origins, and *monogenicists* argued that all human groups derived from the same ancestral geographical origin.[11]

Intuitively, it would seem that polygenicism, in positing independent origins for human races, would be more supportive of racism than monogenicism, which claims one origin. However, as a point of intellectual history, Hume's polygenicism was a milder form of white supremacy than Kant's monogenicism. The connections drawn by Hume did not purport to be necessary, although they were presumed to be permanent. Kant's connections between what he thought was physical race and what we still regard as moral virtues were posited as both necessary and permanent. Richard Popkin claims that polygenicism as well as contemporary theories of racially inherited differences in intelligence need not result in racist doctrines. Popkin cites Frederick Douglass as a prior authority for the general view that strong differences between whites and nonwhites do not abrogate the moral status of nonwhites.[12] While this position of Popkin and Douglass before him is logically coherent and motivated by principles of human justice, its primary concern is racism or egalitarianism, *on a foundation of settled categories of race*. However, when those settled categories themselves are in question, logically and empirically, it is important whether *Homo sapiens* originated in one place or in several geographic locations that correspond to the ancestral origins of groups identified as races in society. In itself, confirmation of polygenicism would have been more supportive of human racial taxonomy than confirmation of monogenicism. However, polygenicism, or the theory of distinct human group origins, has been discredited in biological anthropology since about 1960.[13]

The present consensus in biological anthropology is that all human groups originated from common ancestors in Africa. However, there is considerable disagreement about the length of time groups that are presently on continents other than Africa occupied those continents. Roughly speaking, *out-of-Africa* anthropologists believe that modern humans originated in Africa about 100,000 years ago and began to migrate to other continents about 70,000 years ago, while *multiregionalist* anthropologists argue that after an original migration from Africa, groups evolved on different continents over a period of 1 to 2 million years.

According to the contemporary multiregionalist hypothesis, European, Asian, and African, *Homo sapiens* populations that evolved on different continents after the original African migration evolved as one species, because there was continual gene flow among groups over the history of their evolution.[14] In contrast, the out-of-Africa theorists maintain that *Homo sapiens* probably originated about 500,000 years ago and that all modern humans originated in Africa between 140,000 and 100,000 years ago. On this view, migration from Africa is held to have occurred at the following approximate dates: 70,000 years ago humans migrated from Africa to Asia; 43,000 years ago humans migrated from Asia to Europe; 15 to 50,000 years ago humans migrated from Asia to the Americas.[15] These dates are approximate because recorded human history goes back only 10,000 years, and both the archaeological and biological evidence is incomplete. The out-of-Africa hypothesis is partly based on the unlikelihood of the independent development of the genetic similarities that now exist among African, Asian, European, and American Indian groups.[16] Still, multiregionalist theorists claim that genetic similarities among groups can be accounted for on the basis of *gene flow*, the out-marriage or breeding between members of different continental groups. Multiregionalists calculate that this gene flow need have occurred relatively infrequently, even only once in a generation, to produce the genetic similarities necessary to consider all groups as members as the same evolving species.[17]

Luigi Cavalli-Sforza, who is an out-of-Africa theorist, explains that the longer the period of time a population has occupied a continent, according to archaeological data, the greater the genetic distance, in terms of blood groups and protein polymorphisms, of that population from present occupants of the continent from which it migrated. Thus, blood and protein genetic distance is proportional to the time ancestrally related populations have been reproductively separated from each other. Cavalli-Sforza notes that most nongenetic, or phenotypic data, such as measurements of height and other anthropometric traits, including what are commonly taken to be racial traits, is a less reliable gauge of differences between populations than genetic data, because the anthropometric traits have been influenced by environmental effects on individual development and genetic modification resulting from natural selection (adaptation).[18] In contrast, multiregionalists point out that Cavali-Sforza's equation of genetic distance with the time of reproductive separation between populations is based on an assumption that human continental groups have been reproductively isolated. With gene flow among groups, the relationship of current geographical populations to older populations in the same area need not be a matter of direct descent. Some writers claim that greater genetic distances between non-African and African populations are not the effects of when migrations occurred (which is how the out-of-African theorists interpret the data) but the effects of a larger African population and greater gene flow out of Africa than into Africa.[19]

While natural selection changes the genetic makeup of populations, that kind of genetic change is not useful for determining the ancestral origins of populations. This consideration is highly relevant to attempts to ground racial identity on the geographical location of ancestors, because racial criteria are phenotypical and can be measured only 'anthropometrically.' It also implies that ancestrally close groups might display apparent racial phenotypic differences if present members are descended from populations that had to adapt to very different environments.[20]

To the lay person, the fact that what are taken to be physical racial traits in society are not themselves good indicators of ancestral lineage is paradoxical, especially since the genes for such traits could be identified. But many of those socially designated racial traits are present in soft tissue that cannot be easily reconstructed from osteological (skeletal) remains. Moreover, a major part of the scientific study of human evolutionary history has been to determine the ancestry of what are antecedently taken to be racial groups, and to make the determination in ways that will confirm or disconfirm the antecedent social racial taxonomy. And, it is crucial in studies intended to confirm or falsify the hypothesis that there are human races, that once race has been identified in the ordinary way, other biological traits present in racially identified groups be used to track their lineage over time and distance. This difference in identifying traits and tracking traits protects the race-confirming or race-denying conclusion from being circular; it assures that an assumed taxonomy is not being projected onto those facts that are supposed to be the foundation for the taxonomy. However, there are epistemological problems with the race-identifying or phenotypical traits, and I will address them in chapter 3. Here, it is important to keep in mind that the geographical study of human evolutionary history is not the same thing as confirmation or falsification of the present existence of race. Distinct social races could have geographically distinct ancestry, but that doesn't provide a scientific basis for race, unless there is something scientifically racial about the ancestry.

To return to Cavalli-Sforza's account, the best genetic materials for tracking population lineage are hereditary mutations in genetic material, which have no adaptive function, because they have no protein-producing capability. An apparent exception to this rule is the use by evolutionary theorists of HLA (human leukocyte antigens) gene groups, which are important in human immunology. But, HLAs change as much or more because of chance than natural selection, and it is their frequent, nonfunctional mutations that make them suitable for tracking populations.[21]

Gene frequencies for ABO and RH blood groups, and genes that code for proteins and enzymes, are usually measured within populations. DNA has more recently been used to measure genetic distances between individuals by counting the different mutations in DNA sequences. (DNA is made up of ACG and T nucleotides in different sequences. A complete set of human chromosomes contains 3 billion nucleotides, the human genome.[22]) The Human Genome Diversity Project, begun in the early 1990s, compared world populations that corresponded to social racial groups, for mutational genetic difference. As Cavalli-Sforza relates, all blood protein and DNA marker comparisons result in world trees, within which the greatest genetic difference exists between present occupants of Africa and non-Africans. These measures of genetic difference are usually taken to confirm the "out-of-Africa" thesis about human origins.[23] But multiregionalists argue that the greater genetic distance between Africa and all other populations does not necessarily indicate when population splits occurred, because it could be a result of a larger African population with greater genetic diversity and more gene flow out of it than into it.[24]

Analyses of hereditary blood proteins were used to identify and compare human lineages, both within and between continents, beginning in the 1960s. In the past two decades it has become technologically possible to track descent by the analysis of mitochondrial (mt) DNA. Mt DNA does not break up and recombine in the formation of reproductive cells, as does most other genetic material, but is instead directly passed on by mothers to children. Since women with different mt DNA have different mothers, a mitochondrial lineage is a direct maternal lineage. Mt DNA is subject to a high rate of mutation and is present in each human cell. The date of "Mitochondrial Eve," or "African Eve," the common ancestress of present humans, which Cavalli-Sforza accepts as 143,000 years ago, was arrived at by counting the number of mutations separating Africans from non-Africans and comparing it with the number separating chimps from humans, in calibration with archaeological dating. All females have two X chromsomes, one from each parent. Males have XY, an X from their mothers and a Y from their fathers, so that the Y chromosomes in males can come only from their fathers. Based on a single nucleotide mutation of the Y chromosome, there is also believed to be "African Adam," the common ancestor of present male humans, who lived about 144,000 years ago (and was not a mate of Eve).[25]

Further findings suggest that there were three African Eves, one of whose descendants branched into six Asian Eves, of which one descendant branched into nine European Eves. Several Asian Eve lineages continued directly into the Americas, with no further mt DNA mutations to mark branching. There were three African Adams, one of whose descendants branched into seven Asian Adams, whose lineage continued into Oceania, Europe, and the Americas.[26]

On the out-of-Africa hypothesis, mitochondrial African Eve would be the ancestress of all, both male and female, present humans. But since only males have Y chromosomes, chromosomal African Adam, while the ancestor of all present males, may not have been the ancestor of all present females. (That is, African Adam and his descendants may have mated with the daughters of another Y line that has since passed out of existence.)

The absence of distinct mutations for European male lineages and for both American male and American female lineages is difficult to interpret, beyond the conclusion, based on mt DNA and Y nucleotide mutations, that they have no branches within them. There may or may not have been other genetic changes, not accompanied by identifiable chromosomal mutations, after the time of population migration from Asia to Europe and the Americas. But, as well, there may or may not have been other genetic changes that accompanied the identified genetic mutations for both males and females, during the times marked by distinct mt DNA and Y nucleotide chromosomal lineages.

Finally, relying once more on Cavalli-Sforza, there are microsatellites, short repetitive sequences of DNA, which contain errors or mutations that can serve as genetic markers, because once errors are made in the copying of DNA sequences, during the production of reproductive cells, the errors become a permanent part of DNA sequences. Such errors are the basis for absolute genetic dating, if a rate of mutation can be ascertained. Absolute dating of early humans does not depend on calibration with archaeological evidence, although it places the origins of modern humans in Africa 80,000 years ago, a date that does accord with the independent archaeological data.[27]

Again, multiregionalists dispute that Cavalli-Sforza's and related studies of mitrochondrial Eve support a *recent* African origin of modern *Homo sapiens*, which then populated the rest of the world.[28] The length and details of modern *Homo sapien* history are empirical questions that may be impossible to settle. Still, all contemporary biological anthropologists posit African origins at some point in the past. But, and this is the important point, there is no evidence that African *Homo sapiens* origins are origins of a particular race. None of the genetic data used to reconstruct human natural history relies on racial classifications as they are commonly understood, and neither has this data been shown to have any connection with such classifications. Human origins are by definition geographical and race has been metaphorically associated with geography, but that is far from a causal connection. The out-of-African theorists track human migrations on the assumption that populations can be studied as self-contained breeding units, but nothing in their data or its interpretations supports social racial taxonomies. The multiregionalists reconstruct a longer human history on the presumption of gene flow among populations. They are more likely to make use of anthropometric data in identifying and comparing present geographic populations, but they have less reason to believe that such phenotypic traits have remained the same over the histories of populations in given geographic areas, precisely because of the gene flow among populations that they posit.[29]

The Continuing Lure and Lore of Geography

What does the scientific view of human geographical migration and genetic mutation indicate about the existence of race? Common sense racial categories have a history originating in European colonization of Africa and the Americas, and cultural distance from (if less successful domination of) the Middle East, China, and Japan. Those in the West have divided human groups into biological races, partly on the basis of continental geography, even though the reasons for this division were originally economic, political, and religious. Biological ideas of race were developed in the eighteenth and nineteenth centuries, well after the initial periods of exploration and colonization. (And of course, the process of racial identification was not culturally symmetrical between Europe and its subalterns. The non-European groups who came to have black, Asian, and Indian racial identities imposed on them did not originally consent to those designations, although they developed ideologies of resistance and liberation within intellectual traditions based on reinterpretations of their imposed nonwhite racial identities.[30]) Nonetheless, at first glance the primary cut between Africans and non-Africans in genetic distance and the attendant genealogical branching, with smaller amounts of genetic distance among populations in Asia, Europe, and the Americas seems to support historical and common sense geographical racial taxonomy. But how, exactly?

The consensus that *Homo sapiens* originated in Africa has prompted some writers to claim that the sole human race is the Negro or black one. Lewis Gordon makes this claim as part of his affirmation of black identity in what he calls "antiblack" racist society:

> What the Human Genome Diversity Project reveals is that all human genes originated from the same region: Southeast Africa. During the period of our evolution, when human beings were in a single region, conditions were ripe for the maximum diversity of our gene pool. Subsequent patterns of movement and mating selections led to the focus on certain combinations of those genes in certain regions over others until the gene variations spread across the planet. What this means is that, from a genetic point of view, there is indeed one human species that originated from a single region. But here is the rub: race critics have read this conclusion to mean that races do not exist. In one sense it is true; races do not exist. *One* race exists, and that race is "Negro."[31]

Gordon is here speculating that nonblack racial traits evolved from a totality of racial traits in an original black population. But, until it is independently established on empirical grounds that human races exist, that is, that there are *racial* traits, there is no basis on which to project race onto an original African population, as Gordon does. The original African population may not have had the traits that later came to be associated with all races, or even the traits associated with the presumed black race. There is at present no way to confirm this one way or the other because, as noted earlier, the physical traits associated with race, such as skin color and hair texture, are formations of "soft tissue" for which there is no ancient archaeological record.

There is no reason to believe, as Gordon does—and he has a huge cohort—that geographical distinction alone is sufficient evidence of racial distinction. The Human Genome Diversity Project and other endeavors in molecular genetics do not identify human geographical origins based on what are commonly taken to be physical racial traits, but based on genetic markers, which do no more than accompany population descent, so that migrations and the age of their resulting genealogical lineages can be hypothesized. Thus, suppose that population B, on continent Q, is D genetic distance from population A on continent P. Suppose, also, that the ancestors of B were members of A who traveled from P to Q and that no one in B interbred with members of A who remained on P after the Q-destination ancestors of B left. The number of years that it would take B to develop D genetic difference or 'distance' from A is hypothesized to be the number of years since some members of A left P for Q and formed the new lineage. For out-of-Africa anthropologists, that kind of hypothesis is the only "result" of the available data, and it says nothing about race or racial taxonomy. If the multiregionalists are right, then in the above model, there would have been gene flow between A and B, after some As left P for Q, and that would leave less reason to posit distinctive racial traits in connection with distinctive geographical locations.

The origin of all modern *Homo sapiens* in Africa is consistent with the later development of distinct races or with no racial development. It cannot be claimed, as Gordon does, that the common human origin is proof that there is one human race, namely the black one. Not only is geography alone insufficient to establish the existence of race, but "race" means a taxonomy or division into races. The existence of race is the existence of *races*, of groups generally distinct from each other, on the order of subspecies. If a species were divided into subspecies and all but one became extinct, it could then be said that the species presently had one race. But, this would be true only because of a prior existence of more than one race. Where there is "one race" from the beginning, there are no races. Gordon begs the question of whether there are human races. He extracts one component of common sense racial taxonomy, namely "Negro," and simply projects it onto the scientific description of human origins. This does no more than reinscribe the common sense association of race with geography, which association is itself in need of a scientific foundation, onto a hypothesis about human origins that is not a hypothesis about racial taxonomy. (On top of this projection, Gordon seems to believe that an original "one drop" of African essence has persisted generationally for over 100,000 years![32])

Scientifically oriented mirages of race, based on geography, also now occur in the literature. Cavalli-Sforza's work on population genetics reconstructs the history of human geographical migration out of Africa, in a way that can be modeled through geographical mapping and genealogical branching. Data on linguistic differences between populations can also be modeled in this way, given similar assumptions about migrations and descent, as are made about populations biologically. And, the linguistic mapping and branching appears to coincide with the mapping and branching based on biology.[33] The substantial coincidence of successive geographical populations with common sense continent-based racial categories may seem to fulfill a long promise of a scientific foundation for those categories. But how, exactly?

Robin Andreasen considers the taxonomies of migratory populations that for long periods of time did not interbreed with other populations or with the descendants of their ancestral populations. She suggests that branches of such populations be viewed as *clades*. A clade is an ancestor and descendants, who form an isolated breeding population, which in evolutionary biology, can be used as the unit in models of taxa higher than species. Thus, Andreasen uses the concept of clades to interpret Cavalli-Sforza's data as support for a scientific concept of race.[34] The problem with this proposal is that there is no empirical reason to use Cavalli-Sforza's data as a basis of the common sense concept of race, because his data are based on genetic differences that do not have any known biological relation to those traits that in common sense are associated with race. Cavalli-Sforza and his colleagues selected original subjects for DNA mutational comparison based on a pre-genetic or social classification into black and white racial groups in England and the United States, and membership in over 40 geographically diverse aboriginal groups. The black and white individuals were assumed to have ancestral origins in Africa and Europe, and the aboriginal groups were assumed to have been in their present abodes for long periods of time.[35] Thus, well-founded presumptions about geographical origins were built into the selected categories whose geographical ancestry were to be tracked. But where does race come into this scientific picture, if the common sense racial taxonomy is merely assumed and the geographical origins are not in themselves racial? For instance, if all the people identified as white had ancestors alive in Europe during the same time that the people identified as black had ancestors alive in Africa, to say that these are racial ancestral differences adds no new information to the data on time and place.

Cavalli-Sforza's preselection was made in order to establish genetic base points from which mutations could be identified. The genetic mutational data does not identify race scientifically, but merely identifies likely geographical origins of groups (that is, of the ancestors of selected groups) and paths of population migration. Andreasen is aware of Cavalli-Sforza's own resistance to racialist (that is, entailing belief in the existence of races) interpretations of his data, but she fails to offer an argument against his resistance. The only way Andreasen's races-as-clades proposal could provide a scientific foundation for common sense racial taxonomy is if it is assumed that geography in itself grounds race, so that different ancestral places, even if occupied for only 40,000 or 50,000 years, automatically entails the existence of different races. Skepticism about a scientific foundation for race does not include denial of the ability to prescientifically identify those groups that are presumed to be races—what's at issue is whether the groups are races in any scientific sense. Furthermore, confirmation of the multiregionalist hypothesis would automatically exclude a notion of races-as-clades, because that hypothesis denies the reproductive isolation of human groups. Indeed, if the multiregionalists are correct, no human group that was smaller than the entire species could be a clade.

The question remains open of why geography should be assumed to cause race, or how geographical differences could cause racial differences. A scientific basis for the common assumption that geography causes races would either be a causal explanation of how general or specific racially salient physical traits were linked to geographical conditions, or, coherent statistical support for the conjunction of general or specific racially salient physical traits with some geographical conditions and not others. Geographical origins of ancestors alone could not provide the causal or statistical account, because it is the hereditary effects of geography over time that are supposed to do the racial work. That is, geography is commonly assumed to account for racial differences "as a result of evolution." But this is vague. If *Homo sapiens* has evolved over the past 100,000, 200,000 or 2 million years, adaptive changes are the evidence for it. But what is the evidence that significant and uniform adaptive human changes are correlated with differences in races?

The main apparent difference associated with race—skin color—was until recently believed to be the result of natural selection within populations living under different amounts of sunlight. However, dark-skinned groups live in cold as well as warm climates. The hypothesis that dark skin increases "fitness" in sunny climates, because it offers protection against ultraviolet rays that can cause skin cancer, is undermined by the fact that skin cancer rarely develops in individuals before they are of reproductive age. (That is, in terms of natural selection, fitness means increased reproduction that results from an adaptive trait and not the adaptiveness of individuals independently of whether of not they reproduce.) The hypothesis that light skin facilitates the synthesis of vitamin D in climates with little sunlight is weakened by the fact that there is no evidence of vitamin D deficiency (rickets) in past European populations when winters were more severe, and, also, by recent evidence that vitamin D can be stored in the human body for the length of a northern winter.[36]

However, before skin color differences can be used as evidence for a geographical basis of race, it needs to be independently shown that skin color differences themselves form a taxonomy that corresponds to common sense notions of race. I will address that issue in chapter 3. Here, it can be concluded that the geographical account of human history in itself yields no evidence that modern *Homo sapiens* has evolved in different ways based on groupings that can be defined in racial terms. To repeat, geographical origins do not in themselves constitute races and to assume that they do in the absence of comprehensive supporting human evolutionary data is an egregious bit of flimflam that begs the question of whether or not there are races. Overall, the geographical basis of human racial taxonomy seems to be no more than a rhetorical tradition deriving from Eurocentric reactions to contact with inhabitants of other places. Descriptions of how the inhabitants of Asia, Africa, and America appeared to Europeans during early modern contact are fascinating (and painful) to read, and genetic models of human population migration out of Africa are interesting in their own right as accounts of our species history. But neither type of account yields any more scientific information about race than Amerigo Vespucci's 1503 *Mundus Novis*.

3.
Phenotypes and Ideas of Race

Vertical and Horizontal Models of Human Differences

We saw in chapter 2 that the contemporary account of human geographical migration begins from the assumption that there now exist groups whose ancestral migrations can be tracked. These groups may roughly correspond to common sense races, but the genetic material used to track group ancestry is not the genetic material responsible for those traits considered racial. The ancestral tracking genetic material has no effect on phenotypes, or biological traits of organisms, which would include the traits deemed racial, because the ancestral tracking genetic material plays no role in the production of protein—it is not the kind of material that "codes" for protein production. Neither is there any known mechanism whereby the tracking genetic material causes the racial traits of a person who has distinctive genetic tracking material and distinctive racial traits. Without evidence of any connection between racial traits and genetic tracking material, there is no evidence that populations with the same tracking material, for example, a present population and its ancestral population, have or had the same racial traits. Thus, in itself, the ancestral tracking genetic material is irrelevant to scientific racial identification, definition, or taxonomy, although it is, of course, highly useful for reconstructing the migrational histories of groups.

Genealogical tracking material can be used to support hypotheses about those ancestral groups from which existing individuals and populations descended. The originating ancestral groups are themselves defined by their geographical location at a certain time in the past, and, the geographical location of ancestors is determined by the present location of those presumed to be nonmigratory descendants of the ancestral group. The determination that a population occupies the same geographical location as its ancestors is based on historical records (both written and oral), archaeological evidence, forensic anthropological comparisons between ancient human remains and existing individuals, and absolute atomic dating of ancient human remains.[1] Returning to the example used in chapter 2, suppose that population B on continent Q is D genetic distance from population A on continent P. If we know that B migrated from P, B's ancestors are also the ancestors of A. But since A's ancestors are dead, B must be compared to A on the assumption that A is like its ancestors in the trait being tracked.

Given the four possible empirical bases of ideas of race—geography, phenotype, genotype, and genealogy—it is evident that geography in itself, as mere place, cannot provide a scientific foundation for racial taxonomy. But, of course, 'geography' means more than mere spatial location. 'Geography' includes distinctive environmental conditions that could have an influence on natural selection, because they render individuals with some traits, more likely than individuals lacking those traits, to reproduce successfully and pass on the traits that are beneficial in a given environment. Suppose it can be shown that for a given geographical location, the beneficial and successful traits are identical to, or correlate highly with, hereditary traits that define common sense racial identity. Then, if common sense races corresponded to different ancestral populations, 'geography,' in a broad sense, would be an evolutionary medium for racial taxonomy.

Skin color, or to be more exact, skin shade, or lightness or darkness of skin color, has seemed to be the primary common sense criterion for racial membership and identification. Skin color differences are taken for granted as evidence of racial difference, if not considered to be racial differences in themselves, and skin color is assumed to be the evolutionary result of ancestral geographical environment. But, as indicated at the close of chapter 2, there are problems with using an evolutionary geographical model to explain skin color differences: People with dark skin are present in cold climates, and light skin is not necessarily an adaptive advantage in cold climates that have less sunlight, because recent evidence suggests that vitamin D can be stored in the body. Even more recent evidence suggests that skin color differences around the globe are adaptive responses to the amount of ultraviolet light present. UV light is necessary to produce vitamin D-3 and folate, which support fetal growth, and more of it is absorbed by lighter than darker skin. Too much UV light causes skin cancer, and too little retards fetal growth and bone development. These findings are consonant with the evolutionary racial model but in a way that is too complex to support common sense racial taxonomy, because the shades of human skin color that absorb appropriate amounts of UV light vary continuously over the surface of the globe and do not fall discretely into a fixed number of human groups corresponding to common sense races.[2] UV light is strongest at the equator, and that is where the darkest skin shades are found among indigenous populations; skin shades become continuously lighter with degrees of latitude away from the equator.[3]

There are two important problems with the use of skin color as a basis for race. The first and obvious one is that apart from custom there is no reason to believe that skin color differences are in themselves, or in combination with other biological differences, sufficiently important to provide a basis for a human subspecies, or racial, taxonomy. Structurally, hair and skin are part of the same epidermal systems in mammals, and differences in epidermal coloration within other species are not normally used as a basis for subspecies or racial taxonomies. The second problem is that while skin color is accepted as a foundation for racial difference in society, in nature there are not distinct groups of human skin colors or shades that correspond to common sense racial groups. Furthermore, the geographical continuity of human skin color is not an isolated pattern of human phenotypical difference. ABO blood types also vary continuously on a geographical basis, as do gross morphological traits that are associated with common sense racial differences.[4] In the language of twentieth-century anthropology, the natural referents of common sense racial traits are *clines* and in nature, the traits deemed racial in society, *intergrade*. Charles Darwin was aware of this fact, as was Ashley Montagu. Darwin used it to argue in favor of a common origin for all human races; Montagu used it to argue against the existence of human races.[5]

The geographical continuity among indigenous (or relatively long-dwelling) populations, of those human traits that are criteria for common sense racial distinctions, represents the main problem with the geographical-evolutionary foundation for race, to wit: The identification of distinct, existing, and evident, traits, individuals and populations, supposed to have evolved in different ways, relies on social categories, which presuppose the biological taxonomy that has not yet been established. This is a problem in the epistemology of the *definiendum*. An adequate 'horizontal,' or present-time model of race is necessary, before a 'vertical' evolutionary account of race can be accepted as the cause or explanation of racial divisions or categories that now exist. Although many assume, without argument, that common sense racial groups can be identified in distinctive ways, closer examination of the phenotypical basis of ideas of race precludes a viable 'horozontal' model. The empirical problems with the phenotypical horizontal model is the main subject of this chapter. After I have articulated those problems, I will note their implications for the vertical geographical account of human migrations, discussed in chapter 2.

The Phenotypical Base of Ideas of Race

As stated, the main problem with a horizontal or present-time identification of human races arises from the reality that traits accepted as racial criteria are continuous among, between, and within different social racial groups, and present in all of them; the so-called racial traits do not fall into discrete and mutually exclusive categories as required, in principle, by the common sense taxonomy, but are instead matters of degree. However, the continuity of physical traits deemed racial would not be an insurmountable problem for a racial taxonomy, if the distribution of the physical traits were orderly within the admittedly constructed racial taxonomy. A contrast between light and dark skin as racial criteria, and amounts of hair as a criterion for being bald

or not bald, is instructive in this regard. The claim that there is no distinction (and no 'taxonomy') between being bald and not bald, because there is
a continuum between the two states, is a slippery slope fallacy. If one arbitrarily divides individuals into categories of bald and not bald, everyone in
the not-bald category will have more hair than everyone in the bald category. For a second example, an objection to an arbitrary taxonomy of tall,
medium, and short, which can be imposed on the natural continuum of
human height, might similarly be based on a slippery slope fallacy. With
height, every member of the medium group would be taller than every
member of the short group, and the same would hold for members of the
tall group in comparison to members of the medium group.

The bald–not-bald taxonomy and the tall–medium–short taxonomy
would be arbitrary because the traits measured vary continuously among
human beings, but the divisions within them would be *orderly*. However,
racial division based on skin color are not orderly in the common sense taxonomy of race: If racial division based on skin color were orderly, then every
black person would have darker skin than every white person. (And if Asians
or Native Americans were supposed to have darker skin than whites, then
every Asian and every Native American would have darker skin shades than
every white person.) But, in society, some black individuals have lighter skin
shades than some white individuals, and some white individuals have darker
skin shades than some black individuals. The natural continuum of human
skin shades could be arbitrarily divided into groups in a way that would be
orderly, but this division would not match the common sense racial divisions
that purport to be based on skin color. Skin color, as a primary racial phenotype, is therefore not an empirical basis for common sense racial taxonomy, despite what is generally believed.

Other apparent phenotypical distinctions, such as limb proportion, cranial
capacity, and hair form have served as defining features in racial taxonomies,
either independently or in conjunction with differences in skin color. Yet, it
is difficult to imagine any other observable human phenotype that could take
the place of skin color as a basis for real racial difference. Skin color is not
only easily discernible to adult members of cultures in which skin color differences are believed to be markers of racial differences (if not racial differences in themselves), but it names social racial groups "white," "black,"
"yellow," "red"—in the peculiar blend of literal and metaphorical usage that
characterizes racialist discourse. Even though Darwin did not believe that
evolutionary climactic differences could explain existing differences in skin
color—he thought they were the result of sexual selection—he agreed that
skin color was the most conspicuous and "best marked" indicator of racial
difference.[6]

Still, not all racial phenotypes need be apparent and, indeed, it was widely
believed throughout the nineteenth century that nonapparent ones such as
blood caused the apparent ones in ways that would ultimately be clear to sci-

ence. Nonetheless, all of the beliefs in distinct racial phenotypes have been proved mistaken within twentieth-century science. Those accounts of human differences in skin shade and blood are worth understanding in some detail, because the folk beliefs that skin color and blood determine race are very persistent. Also, it's not as though scientists themselves have always seen through the presumed phenotypical basis of common sense racial taxonomy. On the contrary, they did much to construct and uphold it during the nineteenth and early twentieth centuries.[7] That scientific racialist history, like the essentialism of Hume and Kant, at this time reads like white supremacist doctrine. It is easily critiqued for its racism, even though a good part of its ontology and ignorance to this day persist unchecked both in humanistic scholarly critique and common sense. The racialist (that is, race-positing) residue in contemporary biology and anthropology is less recalcitrant when the facts relevant to race are examined with the same empirical commitment that should have been made when they were first accepted.

A scientific phenotypical basis for race would have at least these requirements. First, the phenotypes would be hereditary traits, but as phenotypes they would be observable traits in existing individuals or groups. Second, it should be possible, based on the observable phenotypical traits, to construct the scientific taxonomy independently of the common sense taxonomy. Third, as a scientific basis for the common sense taxonomy of race, elements of the phenotypical taxonomy ought to correspond to elements of the common sense taxonomy, in consistent and orderly ways.

Skin Color and Race

Human skin colors form a *cline*, which was defined by Ashley Montagu as "a gradient in a measurable genetic character within groups of animals or plants, and correlated with a gradient in the climate, geography or ecology of the groups."[8] The global continuity of human skin shades among indigenous populations suggests that there is no *qualitative* difference within human skin shades that correspond to social races. Indeed, this appears to be the case, although on a micro level of skin structure and physiology, some researchers may describe differences that correspond to racial differences as qualitative, either because the complexity of the processes resulting in different skin shades itself requires a classificatory scheme, or because they project the social taxonomy onto the physiological differences. All of the genes for human skin pigmentation have not yet been conclusively identified, although most writers hypothesize between two and five pairs of genes, which combine in additive ways to produce 'darkness' or high degrees of pigmentation. But, as Alain Corcos reasons, the number of genes hypothesized varies directly with the number of skin color classifications that are first identified. The working formula is that n, the number of genes in a model of the production of skin color, will generate $n + 2$ skin colors.[9] Eventually, research on the human genome should yield a definite number of genes corre-sponding to skin "color." Indeed, a recent study suggests that new statistical genetic methods are useful in determining whether there may be "major genes" for skin shades.[10] However, the capability of tanning among many adults in all skin shade groups, and the varied influence of developmental factors, suggest that any correlation between the skin shades of adults in non-laboratory conditions, with genes for skin pigmentation, will always be imprecise.[11]

Members of all social racial groups have skin pigmentation and there are general accounts of human skin pigmentation. Given the importance of skin color differences in common sense racial taxonomies, contemporary biolo-gists and anthropologists who provide physiological accounts of human skin pigmentation in general, and of its specific differences, have two choices of approach after providing the general account. They can proceed directly to more specific physiological facts about pigmentation, which are associated with differences in skin color, or, they can interrupt the scientific account by using common sense racial taxonomy to pick the subjects for investigation and comparison of the specific ways in which human pigmentation differs on a physiological level. The first approach is mainly theoretical, because those who study human skin pigmentation cannot help but be aware of its racial importance. But if this approach were used, the result would be a sci-entific description of differences in human skin shades that had been objec-tively measured, and which made no mention of common sense racial categories. The second approach is the traditional one that gives the impres-sion of providing a scientific foundation for racial skin color differences. But, this foundation varies directly with the social racial classification that is used as a starting point for the description of the physiological differences in skin pigmentation. It does not provide a foundation for racial taxonomy in any causal sense, but merely a redescription, in the scientific language of human skin pigmentation, of the skin shades of groups or their typical members within the social taxonomy. Thus, the physiological account of human skin pigmentation, either in general terms or in terms of specific differences, fails to explain *racial* differences in skin color. This is because in nature, skin colors (shades) vary continuously over populations, while racial distinctions require a relatively small number of discrete categories. While differences in physiology do cause differences in visible skin shades, they cannot cause any given system of racial classification.

In *The Human Species: An Introduction to Biological Anthropology*, John Relethford presents the facts about human skin color, as follows:

> Skin color is caused by three pigments. One pigment, *melanin*, is respon-sible for the majority of variations in lightness and darkness in skin color. Melanin is a brown pigment secreted by cells in the bottom layer of the

skin. All human populations appear to have the same number of melanin-producing cells. Variations in the darkness of the skin depends on how many cells actually produce melanin and how they cluster together. The more they cluster, the darker the skin color.

Another pigment affecting skin color is *hemoglobin*, which gives oxygenated blood cells their red color. Light-skinned people have little melanin near the surface of the skin and so the red color shows through. Because of this effect, "white" people are actually "pink." A third pigment is *carotene*, a yellowish pigment obtained from certain foods.... Carotene, however, is not responsible for the yellowish hue of many Asian populations. Their coloring is caused instead by a thickening of the outer layer of the skin.

Skin color is also affected to a certain extent by sex and age. In general, males are darker than females, probably because of differential effects of sex hormones on melanin production. Age also produces variation. The skin darkens somewhat during adolescence, particularly in females.[12]

Relethford's textbook account is based on widely accepted research on the structures involved in the development of human skin pigmentation. Delving into the next level of information on the subject, for instance Ashley Robins's *Biological Perspectives on Human Pigmentation*, published in the Cambridge Studies in Biological Anthropology series, we learn that *melanin*, which is responsible for the darkness of skin, is synthesized in *melanocytes* that are situated at the epidermal-dermal junction. In all humans, melanocytes are more densely concentrated in the face and genital areas, regardless of their degree of pigmentation or social racial classification. Melanin is produced in a cytoplasmic organelle, or *melanosome*, which is made up of structural proteins and the enzyme tyrosinase. Four stages in the development of the melanosome culminate in the production of melanin. The melanocytes interact through their dendrites with *keratinocytes* in the epidermis; the transfer of melanosomes, from the melanocytes to keratinocytes causes skin to appear pigmented.[13] There is no chemical difference associated with social race in either the melanosomes or keratinocytes. Robins cites a study in which cell cultures of "Negroid" or "Caucasoid" melanocytes were mixed with cultures of "Negroid" or "Caucasoid" keratinocytes:

> Caucasoid melanocytes donated melanosomes both to Caucasoid and to Negroid keratinocytes and vice versa. In Caucasoid melanocyte–Negroid keratinocyte co-cultures the Caucasoid melanocytes became more pigmented than in Caucasoid melanocyte–Caucasoid keratinocyte co-cultures. This experimental result implies a major feedback mechanism from keratinocytes to melanocytes.[14]

Robins's description of melanocyte-keratinocyte transfer is an interesting example of the use of common sense racial classifications in a scientific context that does not support them. Robins projects racial classification onto the cellular processes to identify the source of the melanocytes in the transfer described above. But, after describing how the "Caucasoid-Negroid" transfer resulted in greater pigmentation than the "Caucasoid-Caucasoid" transfer, he takes this to be evidence only of keratinocyte-melanocyte feedback and not of a transformation of skin color from "Caucasoid" to "Negroid," as his initial projection of the racial classification might imply.

Returning to Robins's account of skin pigmentation, once melanosomes are in the cytoplasm of keratinocytes, they are arranged either as single particles or in aggregates. Small melanosomes become aggregated and subject to lysosomal degradation. Larger melanosomes are singly dispersed. Members of all racial groups (that is, people of all skin shades) have the same number of melanocytes. Differences in pigmentation are a result of the size and number of melanosomes. Smaller, fewer, aggregated melanosomes result in light skin; larger, single melanosomes, which tend to form caps over the nuclei of cells, result in darker skin. Under light microscopy, epidermal scrapings contain more melanosomes for "Negroids" than "Caucasoids." But, it is more difficult to distinguish among light-skinned Negroids, Mongoloids, and deeply tanned Caucasoids. Also, aggregated melanosomes from Mongoloids and Caucasoids have been converted to large single ones, after exposure to ultraviolet light,[15] and both single and aggregated melanosomes occur in all racial groups. Overall, the size of melanosomes is neither invariably correlated with racial groups, nor with the intensity of skin pigmentation; for example, Caddo Amerindians have larger melanosomes than American Negroids with lighter skin shades. Moreover, the keratinocytes of scalp hair bulbs have very large melanosomes in all racial groups. It has been postulated that differences in how tightly packed melanosomes are results in differences in pigmentation: dark skin tends to have singly distributed large melanosomes; light skin, smaller ones in aggregates. Robins concludes that melanosome size is more influential than dispersion, although he notes that there is a dilemma in deciding which of these factors has the dominant influence. Also, melanosomes produce melanin in four stages, leading to pigmentation, and dark skin has more stage 3 and 4 melanosomes than does light skin.[16] Yet, there are additional factors affecting skin pigmentation: the rates of melanosome formation and of melanosome transfer to kerotinocytes; epidermal thickness; dermal blood supply; reflective and absorptive properties of the skin.[17]

While my summary of Robins's description of the physiology of human skin pigmentation is a simplification of the complex processes now known, it shows that there are no consistent qualitative differences corresponding to social races. The large number of variables in the processes also suggests that even though observable pigmentation may vary continuously over the surface of the globe for indigenous populations, the underlying physiological processes and structures may not vary in orderly ways that correspond to the geographical continuity in observable pigmentation. Therefore, even if an orderly racial taxonomy of skin color were constructed, based on the observed geographical continuity of indigenous population skin pigmentation, the underlying physiology and cell structures might not vary in a correspondingly orderly way. But, whether there can be scientific laws or generalizations for the causes of variations in human skin shades is still an open empirical question. It should be noted that much of the research on skin pigmentation differences uses subjects who are first identified by race in common sense terms. Given the variety of skin shades within common sense races, it is impossible to tell how much of the complexity of variation is the result of different researchers classifying people with different skin shades as members of the same race. If all researchers identified their subjects by skin shade, objectively, as based on skin reflectance spectrophotometer readings, the data on the physiology of variation might be easier to use as a basis of generalizations. However, given such objective generation of data, the study of human skin pigmentation would then lose its racial relevance, and probably much of its interest. We need to remember that the problem for scientific skin pigmentation descriptions, as a phenotypical base of race, is insurmountable on the more preliminary level that skin pigmentation varies as much within accepted social racial categories as it does between them. Researchers might be able to find clear distinctions in underlying pigmentation physiology if they compared "typical" blacks with "typical" whites, but such practice would raise questions that cannot be answered in favor of typicality without bias. How is typicality to be determined, and by whom? Why should common sense racial typicality be a starting point for scientific investigation? What would be said about the pigmentation of atypical members of the race that was being studied?

Blood and Race

American folk usage is still rich in metaphorical use of "blood" in association with racial identity, particularly for those now considered nonwhite or whose groups have histories of nonwhite identification, for example, "black blood," "Indian blood," "Chinese blood," and also, "Jewish blood," "Irish blood," and so forth. The blood metaphor is the residue of earlier beliefs that racial essences were inherited in the blood. I will discuss heredity in chapter 4, but in this section, blood types are examined as candidates for a scientific phenotypical basis of race.

Because skin color is a complex polymorphic trait that is highly subject to environmental and developmental influences, not much is conclusively known about its heredity. So, in attempts to describe the physiology of apparent skin colors, it has been difficult to isolate the hereditary effects that could count as racial. Unlike skin color genes, genetic blood type schemes, such as ABO, rhesus, MN, and many others, produce phenotypes, or types of molecules on the surface of red blood cells, which are constant, given differences and changes in environment and development. During the early twentieth century, blood phenotypes were considered to be easily classifiable effects of their presumed genotypes. Also, since people do not select mates on the basis of their blood types, in isolated breeding populations, with no immigration or out-marriage, blood group distribution remains constant.[18] For these reasons, during the first half of the twentieth century blood phenotypes held the promise of providing a scientific racial taxonomy. At the close of a 1943 review of blood group research dating from World War I, Alexander Weiner remarked that "the published data regarding the racial distribution of the blood groups probably exceeds that available for any other anthropological criterion."[19] But in his introduction to the same review, Weiner advanced this conclusion about the data:

> Attempts to produce sera which would serve to differentiate bloods of different races particularly in the human species have been unsuccessful.... Agglutinogens of human blood so far discovered are not restricted to any race, and consequently the presence or absence of any of the agglutinogens in a given blood specimen cannot be used as evidence that the blood came from an individual of a given race. However, the study of the agglutinogens in the bloods of large groups of individuals has shown that their *frequency distribution* varies in different races.[20]

Weiner's conclusion about the lack of correlation between blood types and racial groups and the variation in frequency distribution within common sense races carries the same weight today. To consider these issues more precisely, let's begin with a definition of the most famous blood type group:

> The **ABO blood group system** [is] the most important of the antigens of human red blood cells for blood transfusion seriology. Humans belong to one of four groups: A, B, AB and O. The red cells of each group carry respectively the A antigen, the B antigen, both A and B antigens, or neither. Natural antibodies (resulting from immunization by bacteria in the gut) are present in the blood against the blood group antigen which is absent from the red cells. Thus persons of group A have anti-B, of group B have anti-A, of group O have anti-A and anti-B, and group AB have neither. Before blood transfusion the blood must be cross-matched to ensure that red cells of one group are not given to a person possessing antibodies against them.[21]

We need to remember that the genes for blood groups are the same in all humans; the variation within blood groups, such as ABO, is a difference in allele, or gene type.[22] Also, the foregoing is a definition of ABO phenotypes. The contrast between the ABO phenotypes and their underlying genotypes is usually set out as follows:

Phenotypical Blood Group	Antigen	Antibodies	Genetic Allele
A	A	Anti-B	AA or AO
B	B	Anti-A	BB or BO
AB	A and B	None	AB
O	None	Anti-A and Anti-B	OO[23]

The ABO blood type system is a fraction of the 32 public and private (that is, variable only within single families[24]) blood group systems, which include MN, Rh, Lewis and secretion of ABO antigens, P, Lutheran, Kell, Duffy, Kidd, and others.[25] The frequency distributions of blood types in populations are usually calculated in terms of genotypes, which, traditionally (before the assemblage of the human genome, and the identification of specific genes made possible in recent decades), have been deduced from data on phenotypes, according to Mendelian laws of heredity. However, given the complexity of factors in blood polymorphisms in individuals, precise relationships between genotypes and phenotypes for many blood groups other than ABO and MN cannot be generalized.[26]

Anthropologists who pioneered the use of blood group frequencies within populations, as a tool for defining racial typologies, concentrated on genotypes because they were interested in hereditary data that could be used to ground common sense racial taxonomies in evolutionary and migratory taxonomies of human populations. Thus, with blood groups, as with other scientific investigations of specifically racial taxonomy, the vertical and horizontal models have traditionally been conflated. As Weiner expressed it, the apparent independence of blood group genes from environmental influences was part of its initial promise. This independence and the apparent simplicity with which blood group heredity obeyed Mendelian laws could have resulted in genetic typologies that would have accurately predicted phenotypical typologies of blood corresponding to social racial classification. But, soon into this project, it became evident that there were no uniform classifications of human groups based on blood type frequencies. For most blood group systems, all of their alleles appear in all social racial groups, and there are no uniform variations of alleles, which correspond to social racial groups. The frequencies of blood group alleles also vary locally within social racial subgroups. Furthermore, racial groups with significant frequency differences within a given blood group system do not have predictable differences in allele frequencies for other blood group systems, largely because blood group alleles from one system are inherited independently of blood group alleles from other systems.[27]

As a result of the lack of uniformity in blood research data on race (which followed the lack of uniformity in research on morphological phenotypes associated with common sense races), race was abandoned as a subject in anthropology by the mid-twentieth century, and it was replaced with the subject of "breeding populations." Breeding populations were presumed to be reproductively isolated groups that had distinctive frequencies of selected alleles.[28] Widely quoted in this regard is Alice Brues's definition of a race as "a division of the species that differs from other divisions by the frequency with which certain hereditary traits appear among its members."[29]

The theoretical change to populations instead of races notwithstanding, attempts to use blood allele variations to define distinct populations have not been successful.[30] If distinct populations are defined as groups with different blood allele frequencies, there is no independent way to decide how different the frequencies have to be and which alleles are more definitive. Only the addition of assumed common sense racial phenotypes, such as morphology and skin color could render blood group taxonomies racial. N. P. Dubunin reviewed the literature on such renderings in 1965, and when "other anthropological features" were combined with blood group antigen data, the number of races proposed by leading researchers were 5, 9, 32, or 34.[31] The main problem with these figures is not the implication that any racial taxonomy constructed this way would be arbitrary,[32] but that the "other anthropological features" have not been independently justified as a scientific basis for racial divisions. "Fixing" the racially uninformative aspects of blood-based population taxonomies with the addition of data about "other anthropological features" is a trap one would expect population geneticists to avoid.

Luigi Cavalli-Sforza steers clear of this trap in both the long (1994) and short (1995) forms of his retrospective account of his own research using blood-based data. In 1961 and 1962, when Cavalli-Sforza and Anthony Edwards worked on analyses of blood group data for fifteen populations on five continents, they computed the genetic distance between pairs of populations for ABO, Rh, MN, Diego, and Duffy blood groups. Cavalli-Sforza and Edwards drew an evolutionary tree that showed Ghanaians and Australian Aborigines to be the greatest distance apart. They did not know how to assess their results, which placed Europeans as an intermediary group between Africans and Asians. When they revised these results using anthropometric data on hair and skin color, limb length, skull measurements, and the like, they obtained a tree that placed Australian Aborigines closer to Africans than Asians. But, they did not accept the anthropometric measurements because of their dependence on short-term environmental and climatic conditions. Cavalli-Sforza and Edwards's subsequent research, using a wider range of nonanthropometric genetic factors that included blood groups, enzymes, proteins, and HLAs (human lymphocyte antigens, or proteins on the surface of white blood cells that participate in the formation of antibodies)[33] from 42 world populations resulted in a tree in which the greatest genetic distance appeared to be between Africans and all other groups. However, Cavalli-Sforza states that these results assume constant rates of evolutionary change in the factors being compared.[34] He also states elsewhere that such trees cannot give substance to racial taxonomies, because it is purely arbitrary where racial divisions are drawn, based on historical genetic population branches:

> The classification into races has proved to be a futile exercise for reasons that were already clear to Darwin. Human races are still extremely unstable entities in the hands of modern taxonomists, who define from 3 to 60 or more races. To some extent, this latitude depends on the personal preference of taxonomists, who may choose to be "lumpers" or "splitters." Although there is no doubt that there is only one human species, there are clearly no objective reasons for stopping at any particular level of taxonomic splitting. In fact, the analysis we carry out ... for the purposes of evolutionary study shows that the level at which we stop our classification is completely arbitrary.[35]

Blood and the Racial Project

Blood group phenotypes and genotypes are presumed to be insulated from environmental factors and natural selection. There are two reasons why such insulation is desirable for research. The first is that it enables genealogical studies that are not thrown off by rapid adaptive changes in otherwise closely related populations. The second concerns the scientific racial project. Generally, since its inception, this project has been accompanied by vague implicit assumptions that racial traits are not subject to change, either in individuals or in populations. It is known that biological populations evolve or change over time, so the reason that racial traits are required to be stable must be because of the common sense belief that races are unchanging. The grand triumph of the scientific racial project would have been the discovery of distinct, general race factors that could have been used to account for more specific variations. A smaller victory would have been the discovery of specific biological traits that varied significantly according to social races or even just according to populations. Assume two populations with common ancestry. They could qualify as races if they uniformly differed in at least one genetic trait. *Blood*, or a scientific taxonomy of blood types, was not only, as the metaphoric medium of racial transmission, the last scientific location for anything that could play the role of a racial essense, but it was also the last candidate for anything that could be a racial *accident* or necessary and/or sufficient condition for specific racial identities.

The present understanding of the genetics of sickle cell anemia further undermines the desirability of blood-based research for both genealogical studies and the race project. Sickle cell anemia is a genetic disease in which, because of an abnormal shape, red blood cells are unable to transport hemoglobin. It is coded for by two recessive genes (the homozygous condition). When only one of these genes is present (the heterozygous condition), the individual functions normally; when both genes are present, the individual rarely survives to adulthood. Without external environmental factors, it would be expected that there would be a low frequency of both the homozygous and heterozygous conditions, because those individuals who were homozygous would not live to reproduce and there would be no advantage for those who were heterozygous. However, in areas of southern Africa with the most serious forms of malaria, there are relatively high frequencies of individuals who are heterozygous for sickle cell anemia. It is believed that this is because the heterozygous condition renders red blood cells less susceptible to the malaria parasite, because of an abnormal shape that defeats the malaria parasite, but is not so abnormal that it produces sickle cell anemia.[36] A parallel situation exists with the genes for the disease *thalassemia*, which is present in populations in southern Europe, where malaria also occurs.[37]

In the United States, sickle cell anemia has been publicized as a disease of African Americans, exclusively, following folk notions of racial essences that have the ability to cause racially distinct diseases. Exhibiting a belief about the ontology of races that falls between scientific information and folklore, the Agency for Health Care Policy and Research of the American Medical Association recommended in 1991 that all infants be tested for sickle cell anemia. Their reasoning was that although the disease had a higher prevalence among individuals of African, Middle Eastern, and southern European descent, there were no scientific methods that could determine racial identity.[38] They made a leap from the geographical location of ancestors to racial identity, although they should have known in 1991 that there was no basis for their apparent belief in disease-causing racial identities. Still, it was to their credit that they admitted an inability to clinically determine either geographical ancestry or race.

Anthropological evolutionists have reported that the original presence of the sickle cell allele was probably the result of a mutation. The heterozygous or recessive form of the mutation became advantageous when forest dwelling populations chopped down trees and converted to horticulture, making it possible for mosquitos bearing the malaria parasite to breed in stagnant pools under sunlight.[39] Under those malarial conditions, people homozygous for sickle cell anemia would succumb to that, and people with normal red blood cells could succumb to malaria, so that those heterozygous for sickle cell anemia had the best chances of surviving and reproducing.

What is now known about the advantages of the sickle cell heterozygous condition and the external environmental influences involved make it clear that sickle cell anemia is a disease that could be present in any group that developed the genetic mutation under environmental conditions similar to those in parts of southern Africa. As expected, when the malarial conditions are no longer present, descendants of the African population that has a high frequency of the heterozygous condition exhibit lower frequencies of the heterozygous condition. For instance, African Americans descended from families originally from malarial parts of southern Africa, who have spent generations in nonmalarial environments, have lower rates of the recessive sickle cell condition than their counterparts in the same regions as their ancestors.[40]

Other Racial Phenotypes

Racial skin color differences have always seemed obvious, and blood differences held the promise of providing an objective phenotypical basis for race. We have seen how both skin and blood differences fail to scientifically ground common sense ideas of race. We should now consider what contemporary anthropologists have concluded about other measurable differences associated with social race. Because the failure of anthropometry is already well known and even intuitively understood in humanistic scholarship, it remains only to underscore the inadequacy of what Dubinin called "other anthropological features" to shore up or otherwise supplement scientific attempts to construct a phenotypical taxonomy of race based on hereditary blood group differences. By the mid-twentieth century, C. Loring Brace neatly summarized the anthropological consensus about how presumptively racial features should be understood: "The most important thing for the analysis of human variation is the appreciation of the selective pressures which have operated to influence the expression of each trait separately."[41]

According to Brace, hair color varies directly in pigment with skin color, perhaps less for adaptive reasons than for the fact that hair itself is a structure developed from the epidermis. Thick and curly hair form can be understood as providing insulation from high degrees of exposure to solar heat radiation. Brace explains the variation in human tooth size with reference to different environmental and cultural conditions causing wear, so that large teeth, which take longer to wear down, are favored where it is necessary to use teeth as tools. The geographical or population distribution of human tooth size is not correlated with the distribution of skin shade. Brace also relates nose length directly to extremely dry or warm conditions. Both small size and elongated body shape make it easier to dissipate body heat in high temperatures, while large round bodies have greater volumes relative to their surface, which conserves heat in cold climates.[42] (Cavalli-Sforza, writing over thirty years, later published similar reflections about body size in a discussion about African pygmies.[43])

Such evolutionary accounts of human variation, even if the variation is taken to be racial in ordinary life, are far removed from the construction of scientific racial phenotypical taxonomies that were common in the nineteenth century. The focus then was on cranial capacity and by speculation, brain size, in conjunction with the belief that intelligence varied directly with brain size. Stephen Jay Gould's work, beginning in the early 1980s, of debunking such anthropometry, is justifiably acclaimed.[44] It is also important to remember that the nineteenth-century scientists of race began with strong, value-laden assumptions about the existence of races and then attempted to use measurements as proof of their antecedent bias toward white superiority.[45] Regarding the relation of cranial capacity to brain size, intelligence, and other high attainments, Montagu summed it up very nicely: "What the racist never mentions is that the average volume of the brain of Neanderthal man was 1550 cubic centimeters—150 cubic centimeters greater than that of modern whites!"[46]

To conclude, the variable phenotypical anthropological traits, like skin color and blood, which may be considered racial traits in common sense, cannot be a phenotypical basis for race in science. They vary independently within social racial groups and neither singly nor together do the variations fall into discrete groups that can be correlated with social racial categories. Perhaps more important than these taxonomic problems, human phenotypical variations represent evolutionary adaptations, many of which are very local. Such changing traits within populations, and the presence in every population of traits that could in principle be present in any population, undermine the division into groups, uniformity within groups, and permanence of groups, connoted by the traditional concept of race.

The Vertical and Horizontal Models Contrasted Again

Now, let's return to the geographical history of human migration, as a temporally vertical model of human difference. As explained earlier, for the vertical model to succeed as a geographical migratory account of race, it should be possible to identify races, independently, in a horizontal or present-time model, based on their phenotypical differences. But, the horizontal phenotypical model of race is incoherent and without scientific support. Given the failure of the phenotypical racial model, there is no basis on which to pick out or identify the racial groups whose ancestral migration can be tracked. Therefore, there are no grounds on which to believe that the vertical model is an account of race or common sense racial distinctions.

However, the failure of a horizontal model of race does not impugn a vertical model of human variety. Some of the traits society uses to identify people on the basis of race are instances of real biological variety among *Homo sapiens*. Those traits, without their social overlay as racial traits, can be used in the vertical model to initially identify populations living in the same place as ancestors believed to have migrated from known starting points. Of course, beyond that initial identification, groups would be identified by genetic material having no relation to any phenotype or somatic trait. Thus, the vertical model remains of great importance and interest as a series of big historical narratives about events that preceded recorded history, and conditions that predated what is (mistakenly or not) considered to be human civilization.

4.
Transmission Genetics and Ideas of Race

Race and Heredity

In chapter 1, it was evident that even the Enlightenment philosophers Hume and Kant did not, beyond assuming the existence of human races, provide a conceptual justification for social racial taxonomy. I showed how Kant relied on a notion of racial essences that was metaphysical and as such not useful for an empirical scientific basis of race, and how Hume's assumptions about white supremacy would have required a similar essentialism, in contradiction of his empiricist philosophical commitments. In chapter 2, I examined the geographical basis of race, and it became clear that neither geography itself, nor geography combined with some adaptive evolutionary changes, can ground 'race.' In chapter 3, I addressed the phenotypes associated with race, as a possible scientific basis for social racial typology. The two most important phenotypes in racial identification, skin shades and blood types, were seen not to correspond with social racial categories. The late-nineteenth- and early-twentieth-century attempts at scientific anthropometry yielded no other phenotypes that came close to blood types in a promise of objectivity or otherwise corresponded with social racial categories. The failure of a phenotypical basis for race entails the failure of the hypothesis that phenotypic differences between social races are the evolutionary effects of differences in environmental conditions, because the apparent phenotypic differences in social races cannot be translated into scientific generalizations. There is too much phenotypic variety within social racial groups to scientifically identify those groups based on phenotypes.

In this chapter and the next, I will examine possible scientific bases for hereditary ideas of race. There are two ways that race seems to be hereditary. First, physical racial traits are hereditary traits and therefore to a large extent determined by genes. Second, an individual's racial membership is usually taken to be the result of the racial membership of his or her parents and ancestors. The first kind of racial hereditary, did it exist, would have to be confirmed by *transmission genetics*, which accounts for the inheritance of specific biological traits. The second kind of racial hereditary is *genealogical heredity*. Genealogy has a macro and micro level. On the macro level, an evolutionary group spanning millennia could provide a genealogical grounding of race if it had distinctive common ancestry. On the micro level, genealogy describes how, within time frames in social, recorded history, individuals are related to each other through parents, ancestors, and collateral kin (relatives descended from common ancestors in different parental lines of descent). Both macro and micro genealogy concern relations of entire organisms and not simply their specific biological traits. The subject of this chapter is transmission genetics as a hereditary basis for race. Genealogy, on both levels, is addressed in chapter 5.

Mendelian Heredity

An adequate explanation of the current state of the art of molecular genetics and its theoretical development over the last century would overflow many volumes several times the length of this one.[1] But a few textbook-type facts about genetic transmission will not take long to remind the reader.

The hereditary material of plants and animals is contained in *DNA*, the molecule deoxyribonucleic acid. DNA functions as a set of programs for the development, growth, and physiological functioning of living things. It has the structure of a double helix ladder, the rungs of which are chemical bases. These bases combine with amino acids present in living cells to form proteins, the basic physical material of all living things. DNA is mainly contained within the nucleus of each cell, except for mitochondrial DNA, which is responsible for cellular metabolism. Molecules of ribonucleic acid, in the form of *messenger RNA* and *transfer RNA*, convey duplicates of the specific structures of DNA to other parts of cells for protein synthesis.

Genes, those parts of DNA that determine the development of hereditary traits, are segments of *chromosomes*, or long strands of DNA. At present, there are believed to be between 30,000 and 40,000 genes in the human genome.[2] All human beings have the same genes, but they differ in their *alleles*, or forms of those genes, as well as in the part of human DNA, which does not consist of genes. Based on group comparisons of mitochondrial DNA (inherited from mothers) and Y chromosome DNA (inherited from fathers), neither of which contain protein-coding information, and nuclear DNA (inherited from both parents), which does contain protein-coding information, the overall difference within the human species is believed to be 0.2 percent of all human genetic material, or 1/500. Of that 0.2 percent difference, 90 to 94 percent falls within social racial groups and 6 to 10 percent, or between 1/8000 and 1/5000 of all human genetic material, occurs between races. Most of human genetic variation—no less than 90 percent—occurs locally, between any two people who happen to be neighbors. Another way of putting this is to point out that all human subgroups contain almost all of the *Homo sapiens* species variation within their members.[3] Although, of course, the specific part of the total species variation not contained in a subgroup would differ among subgroups.

Genes, or rather their allelic forms, are identified by their *loci* or locations on chromosomes. Human beings have 23 pairs of chromosomes and typically, each pair has two alleles for the loci of the gene in question. The alleles of a gene may be the same or different. If they are the same, the phenotype, or trait of the person, will be the same as the genotype. For example, in the case of the ABO blood group system, someone with AA alleles, or the AA genotype, will have type A blood, as a phenotype. If the alleles are different, one may be dominant and the other recessive, in which case the phenotype will be determined by the dominant allele, while the recessive allele will be suppressed in the phenotype. Again in the ABO system, someone with an AO genotype will have an A phenotype, because the A allele is dominant and the O allele is recessive. Different alleles, for example M and N in the MN blood type system, may be codominant, in which case both will be expressed, so that someone with an MN genotype will have an MN phenotype. Some alleles affect the expression of alleles in loci other than their own, and some phenotypes are the result of more than one allele pair, for example, skin color.[4] Overall, the expression of alleles in phenotypical traits is the combined result of the alleles, other alleles, the internal physical environment of the organism, the external environment, and apparently random factors in development.[5]

Cells replicate themselves during the development and life of an organism through the process of *mitosis*. During mitosis, within the cell nucleus, chromosomes first duplicate themselves and form new nuclear membranes. The duplicated cell then separates, so that one cell becomes two, each of which has 23 pairs of chromosomes, the standard number for *Homo sapiens*. During *meiosis*, or the formation of reproductive cells (eggs and sperm), the process is more complex. A cell first reproduces by duplication and splitting, as in mitosis, but the resulting two cells further divide so that there are four reproductive cells, each one of which has only one of each of the 23 chromosome pairs, or 23 chromosomes instead of 46. That is, each sperm and each egg has only half the number of chromosomes characteristic of the human species. The 23 chromosomes in an egg or sperm cell contain only one of the alleles at each loci that were present in the cells of its adult parent. During meiosis, one or the other of each chromosome in a pair will go to a reproductive cell. Each pair of chromosomes divides in this way, independently of how the other chromosome pairs divide in forming the reproductive cell. Thus, although any individual will have received half of his or her chromosomes from each parent, it is undetermined which half will be duplicated in any reproductive cell produced by that individual. Also during meiosis, the chromosomes sometimes twist and break, and *cross over*, so that the resulting chromosome going into the egg or sperm has some of the individual's paternal loci along part of its length, with the individual's maternal loci making up the remainder.[6] The same process will have occurred in the conception of the individual, with the result that a person's reproductive cell may have genetic material from her grandfather, her grandmother, or both grandmother and grandfather, even though the reproductive cell has only half as much genetic material as is present in all the other cells of the person's body.

The possibility for variation, as a result of meiosis, is great enough on the basis of just chromosomal combination for there to be millions of genetically unique offspring between any two parents. John Relethford points out that the random division of chromosome pairs during meiosis allows for 2^{23} or 8,388,608 possible sex cells, and any two parents could produce a maximum of 70,368,744,177,664 genetically unique offspring.[7] Since there are no general genes for race, but merely specific alleles of genes for those traits considered racial, the possibilities for inherited variation in apparent racial traits are also very large. For example, if there were only two alleles for each of three racial traits (an oversimplification given accepted social racial taxonomy) that in itself would result in 27 different "racial types."

There is no mechanism in human heredity whereby any of the cultural or historical experiences associated with racial identity can be biologically inherited. Neither is there a mechanism whereby acquired physical characteristics, skills, or traits can be inherited. DNA affects nonnuclear cellular function but is not affected by it (unless reproductive cells are directly altered or mutation occurs). And perhaps most important for an understanding of the mechanism of heredity, each allele is a discrete entity that separates and recombines with other alleles at conception, and maintains its integrity during meiosis. Apparent phenotypical continuity in so-called racial traits is not caused by the "blending" or "mixing" of genes if parents have different traits, but either by the fact that some traits, such as skin color, are *polygenic*, or dependent on more than one gene, or by the expression of recessive alleles that in earlier generations were suppressed by dominant alleles.[8] Some alleles that occur along the same stretch of chromosome may tend to be inherited together, but all loci on chromosomes are subject to recombination during the crossing-over phase of meiosis.[9]

There is no room in the current Mendelian account for a concept of racial essences or specifically racial genes. Such things would have to be major genes or loci controlling a number of phenotypes, and all of the phenotypes associated with race vary independently, which means that their underlying genes also vary independently. In other words, *the evidence of phenotypic variability logically precludes the possibility of general race factors, as well as specific ones.* However, pre-Mendelian theories of heredity would have allowed for the notion of racial essences. Besides physical racial essentialism, there were other pre-Mendelian ideas relevant to race that are interesting to consider, both as factors in the history of science and as the source of beliefs about race that still persist in common sense, even though they have now been falsified by science. Let us therefore focus on several of these earlier scientific notions.

Earlier Scientific Heredity and Contemporary Race

In chapter 1, I discussed Aristotelian essentialism as a metaphysical concept that was presumed to refer to physical parts or aspects of living organisms. Aristotelian essences would have determined the kind of organism that any living thing was, or the species to which it belonged. Thus, although the Aristotelian essence was believed to be present in each individual, it was a species essence. Ernst Mayr, Alan Goodman, and other historians of biology have noted that the ancient concept of essences as applied to biological species was combined with the early Christian idea of a "great chain of being," whereby all of God's created creatures were hierarchically ranked, with the "highest," or spiritually best, closest to God.[10] This combination of ideas was evident in the racial taxonomies in Buffon's *Historiae Naturelle* and Linnaeus's *Systema Naturae*, which were both highly influential throughout Europe during the second half of the eighteenth century.[11] That is, essentialist notions of species seem to have been easily projected onto subspecies, or racial 'taxa.'

The projection of species typology onto racial typology is present in early anthropology, even though anthropologists at that time thought that races were subspecies, rather than species. To this day, the same unexamined projection is contained in connotations of the social term 'race.' To see how this is so, consider, first, Mayr's list of post-Linnaean species characteristics:

(1) species consist of similar individuals sharing in the same essence; (2) each species is separated from all others by a sharp discontinuity; (3) each species is constant through time; (4) there are severe limitations in the possible variation of any one species.[12]

Mayr is not addressing race in his discussion of the history of the species concept. Indeed, the term 'race' does not even appear in the index of his 972-page *Growth of Biological Thought*.[13]

However, to this day, racialists assume the following:

(1) races are made up of individuals sharing the same essence; (2) each race is sharply discontinuous from all others; (3) races maintain their identity across generations ("through time"); (4) there are limitations to the possible variations within races.

Interbreeding among members of different races has always been acknowledged to be possible, not just among human beings, but among different animal races, whereas this is not generally true of different species in the same family. Therefore, the differences between species in the same family are greater than the differences between races. It follows from this that the criteria for the individuation of species cannot be the same as the criteria for the individuation of races. Therefore, whatever used to be believed true of species differences ought not to have been assumed to be true of differences between races. But even if the nature of species differences could hold true for racial differences, whatever may have been believed true of species differences, which is now known to be false, cannot be true of human races (did they exist).

A further aspect of early species essentialism as projected onto racial taxonomies was what both Goodman and Mayr identify as Platonic essentialism.[14] Philosophers tend not to dwell on Plato as an essentialist because they reserve that term for Aristotle, mainly because philosophical terms are often defined as they were used in the history of philosophy, and Aristotle's location of essences in individuals became the dominant medieval version of essentialism and the doctrine problematized by John Locke and other early modern philosophers of science.[15] Aristotle's notion of essences in living things can now be understood as programs for their development, which, as Mayr suggests, is not unlike the contemporary concept of a species genome.[16] In contrast, as understood by biologists, Platonic essentialism was a belief in ideal or otherworldly, perfect types or *forms*. The forms made it possible for actual objects resembling them to exist.[17] This kind of Platonic idealism lingers in folk discourse and behavior related to race, in aversion or preferences for individuals believed to be "typical" of their races in appearance and behavior, and in stereotyping generally. Platonic racial ideals are also evident in introspective searches for authentic racial identities, as defining and validating aspects of the self.

Attributes of white blood, black blood, Asian blood, Jewish blood, and Indian blood, and the use, as nouns, of "half-blood," "full blood," and "bloods" persist in contemporary folk discourse. In chapter 3, the failure of any of the 32 human blood type systems to provide an anthropometric or phenotypical description of social racial taxonomy was examined. The main problem was that heritable blood types within the blood type groups varied independently of each other and other physical racial traits, both within racial groups and in comparisons of racial groups. The early-twentieth-century studies of blood type systems occurred after Mendelian heredity had become widely accepted. Before Mendelianism, blood itself was believed to be the literal medium of hereditary material, not just for race, but for all mammalian heredity.

The idea of blood as the medium of animal inheritance was oddly compatible with the knowledge of the existence of eggs and sperm, a result of Aristotle's postulation that semen was a special state or form of blood. During the development of the genetic theory of inheritance throughout the nineteenth century, blood was still supposed to be the medium through which germ cells traveled. Thus, Darwin in his *pangenesis* explanation of inheritance, postulated that genetic material traveled through the blood to eggs and sperm, from the parts of the body for which it was the specific hereditary material.[18] The restriction of hereditary materials to cell nuclei, the eventual identification of chromosomes, and the identification of genes for different blood groups made it conclusively evident that the blood theory of inheritance was not merely false, but impossible.[19] Blood is no more than somatic tissue, which itself is largely determined by genes.

Pre-Mendelian notions of fractional inheritance and blending are also worth noting for their persistence in contemporary folk belief. Francis Galton, Darwin's younger cousin, is best known for his influence on the development of nineteenth-century eugenics programs. But besides his concern for maximizing the opportunities of "the more suitable races or strains of blood,"[20] Galton was a careful quantitative empiricist who did extensive studies on statistics of variation within human populations. In order to account for apparent regression toward population means in traits such as height, he theorized that every person received one-half of his or her hereditary endowment from each parent, one-fourth from each grandparent, and so on. The idea that ancestral contributions were halved in each successive generation became known as "Galton's law of ancestral heredity."[21] Galton's law was used during the nineteenth century to identify fractions of "black blood," as in 'mulatto,' 'quadroon,' and 'octoroon.' It is still used, not only in racial discourse, particularly about so-called mixed race, but in other discourse about ancestry, such as ancestral national origin in the United States, for instance, when a person refers to herself as "half- Jewish," or "half Irish and half Italian."

The pre-Mendelian notion of blending, also, is still applied throughout hereditary discourse, but most strikingly in discussions of mixed race. Thus, children are said to be "blended" if their parents are of different races. C. Nageli, the preeminent biologist during the time Mendel conducted the research leading to his conclusion that heritable materials or genes maintain their individual integrity across generations, propounded a theory of pure blending inheritance, whereby parental hereditary material was presumed to fuse in procreation.[22] That people still speak of blending in cases of mixed race strongly suggests a generally pervasive pre-Mendelian perspective on race.

Finally, we need to consider the eighteenth- and nineteenth-century theory of *soft inheritance*, which was applied to all heritable traits, generally, and to race in particular ways that still linger. Soft inheritance was the belief that acquired traits, based on the individual organism's experience, are hereditary. It was widely assumed, in all early racial taxonomies, that the cultural and psychological traits of different groups were inherited by each one of their members.[23] It would follow from this that traits developed through psychological, cultural, and moral experiences, as well as skills attained, could become part of an individual's hereditary material. Thus, many racialist and racist assumptions that the greatness or misery and virtue or vice of ancestors are inherited by their descendants have old scientific roots in the doctrine of soft inheritance. (Although this is not to say they lack older roots, such as the biblical notion of the inheritance of the sins of ancestors.)

As Mayr chronicles the stages of the refutation of soft inheritance, every attempt to offer evidence for the doctrine failed. Furthermore, the development of evolutionary theory and the Mendelian genetic theory made it increasingly plausible to explain apparent cases of soft inheritance via the adaptive value of traits determined by constant genes, that is, through hard inheritance. However, Darwin himself allowed for soft inheritance through *pangenesis*, his speculative hypothesis that changes in somatic cells drifted to reproductive cells. Darwin also believed that many generations of disuse would result in a change in the genetic material of the trait or structure that was not used.[24] Different versions of this theory have been traced back to Hippocrates and Darwin was aware of the length of the tradition.[25] Positive refutation of soft inheritance ultimately became available in the 1950s when molecular genetics was used to demonstrate that protein, the stuff of somatic biological experience, has no effect on nucleic acid, the stuff of heredity.[26]

It is not surprising that at the time they were accepted by scientists, mistaken beliefs about inheritance were applied to notions of race and racial distinctions. I can also understand, to an extent, earlier projections of species-type differences onto subspecies or races. But I find it impossible to understand why the falsified scientific ideas about inheritance in general have been so recalcitrant in popular ideas about race. Indeed, almost all of the beliefs about racial difference that are today considered racist derive from discarded notions of human heredity in the general sense. This recalcitrance in matters of race is ironically tragic when perpetuated and vociferously defended by members of nonwhite groups about their own identities, in ways intended to be liberatory.

Race and Population Genetics

Suppose, for the sake of argument, that the search for a genetic basis of race could properly begin with an acceptance of social racial categories. Such grounding would be the weakest possible genetic grounding for race, because it would do no more than enable the redescription, in the scientific language of genes, of some of the criteria for those categories. The genetic redescription alone could not provide a causal explanation of racial distinctions, and neither could it justify the choice of a social racial typology insofar as it were agreed that this typology did not delineate biologically important human differences. Also, the criteria for components of social racial typologies notoriously change, both historically and culturally. For instance, as Alan Goodman notes, southern Europeans, Jews, and Irish were not considered white in the United States until well into the twentieth century, and contemporary definitions of whiteness vary between North and South

America.[27] And, as Joel Williamson and others have chronicled, it wasn't until the late nineteenth century that any degree of black ancestry was a sufficient condition for black identity in the United States.[28] Therefore, any description of racial traits in terms of underlying genes would have to be relative to a specific social typology. Still, if a genetic redescription of apparent racial biological difference could be mapped onto a social typology of race, many people would accept it as some kind of scientific basis for race.

The international consortium that published the first draft sequence of the human genome did not mention or in any way make use of racial taxonomies in their paper. This publicly funded consortium and Celera Genome Corporation, a private concern, independently cloned the three billion bases in the human genome in a competition that appears to have rivaled the discovery of the helical structure of DNA for dramatic development and biological significance.[29] The preliminary conclusion is that humans have a relatively small number of protein-coding genes—30,000 to 40,000—which is only twice the number in the common fruit fly or worm. Human genetic material accounts for less than 1.5 percent of the human genome, the remainder being made up of so-called junk DNA. Much of the human genome consists of genetic information from earlier stages of animal evolution, and it even contains *transposed* bacterial genes. The complexity of human beings is supposed to be the result of combinations of vertebrate-specific protein domains and designs, that is, of the *proteome*. There are also believed to be different ways in which the same gene can be expressed in proteins.[30]

The human evolutionary or historical material contained in the human genome sequence provides a more complete source of genetic information than mutations previously found in mt DNA, Y chromosomes, blood proteins, and nuclear DNA. This allows for more comprehensive comparisons of DNA among populations, for support of hypotheses about human evolution and the migration of ancestral groups. That information and its interpretations are emerging so rapidly that reports often appear in daily newspapers before they are available on the Internet, much less in academic print. As of this writing, the Associated Press reports that Eric Lander, director of the Whitehead Institute at the MIT Center for Genome Research, believes that his study of comparisons of 300 chromosomes from people in Sweden, Central Europe, and Nigeria shows that Europeans are descended from a few hundred ancestors who left Africa as recently as 25,000 years ago. Eddy Ruben, head of the Human Genome Center at the Laurence Berkeley National Laboratory at the University of California, Berkeley, concurs with Lander. Ruben states that although the human species now numbers over six billion, it has the genetic variety of a population of a few tens of thousands.[31] Lander has also been quoted to this effect, both before and after the sequencing of the human genome: "We really are a tiny species grown large in the blink of an eye."[32] While the sequencing of the human genome was in progress, J. Craig Venter, head of Celera Genome Corporation, explicitly stated that race and the human genome are unrelated: "Race is a social concept, not a scientific one. We all evolved in the last 100,000 years from the same small number of tribes that migrated out of Africa and colonized the world."[33] (Although, a genetic population of tens of thousands might have equated in census terms to a population of several hundred thousand, there is no doubt about the general magnitude of our species numerical increase over the course of its rapid evolution thus far.[34])

Nevertheless, an apologist for a genetic racial basis might insist that the apparent consensus about the nonracial aspect of the human genome exists only because the current genome sequence is still a draft and the specific genes underlying traits considered to be racial in society have not yet been individually identified and correlated with those traits. The racialist apologist might also insist that once these genes and their alleles are identified, they will be sufficient to define racial identity, provided that the alleles occurred at different rates in different human groups. In other words, the apologist for scientific racialism would have to retreat to population genetics.

This was in fact the retreat mounted by many biological anthropologists after the middle of the twentieth century. Audrey Smedley, Alan H. Goodman, and others have recounted attempts to ameliorate the failure of the anthropometric, that is, phenotypic, base of race, by replacement of the concept of race with the concept of populations.[35] Widely quoted in this regard is Alice Brues's definition of a race as "a division of a species which differs from other divisions by the frequency with which certain hereditary traits appear among its members."[36] George Gill is also often cited for his claim that a population concept replaced earlier typological thinking as a (scientific) basis for 'race' :

> Confusion and ambiguity surrounding the controversial four letter word "race" was alleviated greatly by the early 1950s following the classic work of Coon, Garn and Birdsell (1950). . . . [T]he underlying basis for the race concept (and racial taxonomy) has shifted entirely in recent decades from a typological to a population one.[37]

However, as Goodman points out, the substitution of 'population' for 'race' is conceptually erroneous, because races are nonevolving, ideal types, whereas populations constantly evolve in response to immediate environmental pressures.[38] Furthermore, the concept of a population is more broad than the concept of a race. A population can be defined as any multi-generational group that is sufficiently isolated to breed within itself. Typically in human history, such isolation has been geographical, but social forms of isolation can give rise to distinct populations that are geographically close enough for their members to interbreed. Geographical or social intra-breeding populations are convenient units for the study of transmission genetics. For example, Luigi Cavalli-Sforza relied on them for early data on human genealogy, which eventually led to the out-of-Africa thesis.[39] And, before the technology for the direct study of the human genome was developed, populations provided extensive data on the transmission of hereditary diseases such as sickle cell anemia and Tay-Sachs.[40] Populations are also excellent sources for the identification of *HLAs* (*human leukocyte antigens*) that are useful for narrowing the field of possible tissue donors for bone marrow transplantation.[41] Nonetheless, the conceptual differences between what are believed to be races and what can be accepted as populations are too great to allow for the substitution of 'population' for 'race.' As a theoretical concept, the notion of a population is not epistemologically tidy. For instance, there are no generally accepted answers to the following questions: How many generations of isolation are necessary to form a population? How large must a population be? What proportion of population members must reproduce in a given generation for it to qualify as a breeding unit? How much gene flow into or out of a group can take place before the population is a different population?[42]

There is a difference between the concept of a population as a substitute for the concept of a race, and the concept of a population in the wider sense as a breeding group. Populations as breeding groups are far more numerous than would be accepted by even the most ambitious racial taxonomists. There is no coherent explanation of what makes one population, such as inhabitants of sub-Saharan Africa, a race, while another breeding group, such as Protestants in Ireland, would fail to be considered a race. As a result, the concept of a population could not take the place of the concept of a race without presupposing and borrowing from the scientifically ungrounded racialist taxonomy that the population concept is supposed to replace.

The concept of a population probably works best when specific historical groups who were reproductively isolated for long stretches of time are the objects of study. However, as hereditary units, populations are groups of individuals, *considered as groups*. The percentage of distinctive biological traits within populations is rarely 100 percent. A trait percentage of 75 percent would mean that 25 percent of the population lacked the trait in question. Populations are rarely surveyed in their entirety for heritable traits, although the larger and more representative the sample considered, the higher the probability that the percentage of the trait in the sample will approximate the percentage of the trait in the population as a whole. Still, what is true of a population as a whole does not apply to each individual member.

If there were reproductively isolated groups in the past that seem to have coincided with what would be considered races in society today, that referent of 'race' is not easily translated into contemporary notions of race. Contemporary notions of race are intended to refer to individuals, as well as groups. Furthermore, if a group has a distinctive percentage of hereditary traits that are considered racial, social questions arise concerning the maintenance of that percentage of the racial traits. The rights of individuals have been the subject of social justice for nonwhite racial groups over the past century, particularly in the American civil rights, voter rights, and immigration rights legislation of the 1960s.[43] Not the least of these rights has been the abolition of laws against marriage between whites and nonwhites. The judicial foundation for not prohibiting interracial marriage was individual rights doctrine. In *Loving v. Virginia*, the landmark case against antimiscegenation laws, U.S. Supreme Court Chief Justice Earl Warren wrote in the majority opinion that marriage was a basic social liberty that could not be regulated on the "invidious" basis of race alone. And this opinion overrode the state of Virginia's argument based on the "desireability of racial integrity."[44]

Racialism after Genetics

Let's return once more to the hypothetical racialist who now knows about Mendelian genetics and human genome sequencing, but who continues to believe that race has or could have a scientific basis in genetics. It could happen at some future date in a racist society that parents might select the race of their unborn children by choosing to alter those genes that code for phenotypical traits that are identified as nonwhite in society. Thus, phenotypically nonwhite parents might choose to have phenotypically white children, to secure social advantages for them. Adults who were phenotypically nonwhite might elect to have gene therapy that would change their racial appearance, for the same social reasons. This would be the future that Frantz Fanon alluded to when he wrote about scientific "denegrification" research, in *Black Skin, White Masks*.[45]

One can imagine the reactions of whites who valued racial purity, and nonwhites who valued racial authenticity—with purity and authenticity now reduced to percentages of racial traits in populations—against such genetic manipulation. On sophisticated levels, both groups would have representatives to argue, as Fanon substantially did, that physical racial changes were an unprincipled reaction to white racism. In the background of the social argument would be an unexamined assumption that race itself had a basis in science, simply because traits falsely believed to be racial could be genetically manipulated. That is, the existence of viable technology would strengthen beliefs in the imaginary object of technology. Even the scientific identification of genes underlying traits believed to be racial now lends substance to the belief that race is real, for those who already assume that race has a basis in science. In a recent *Atlantic Monthly* account of contemporary genetic research, the author not only insisted that the genome revealed information about racial traits and racial groups, but suggested that the scientists associated with the project were dishonest about what they were doing, out of fear of public reaction:

Genetics research is demonstrating that the differences in appearance among groups are profoundly incidental, but these differences *do* have a genetic basis. And although it's true that all people have inherited the same genetic legacy, the genetic differences among groups have important implications for our understanding of history and for biomedical research. The NIH [National Institutes of Health] has been collecting information about genetic variants from different ethnic groups in the United States but it has refused to link specific variants with ethnicity. Celera has been sequencing DNA from an Asian, a Hispanic, a Caucasian and an African-American, but it, too, declines to say which DNA is which.

This strategy of avoiding the issue is almost sure to backfire. It seems to imply that geneticists have something to hide.[46]

If geneticists are hiding anything, it is probably their belief that phenotypic human difference does not support the social racial taxonomy taken for granted as real by the *Atlantic Monthly* author and his public. If there are no racial phenotypes to begin with, then there cannot be any racial genotypes, because effects not in evidence cannot be presumed to have causes. I do wonder why the geneticists in question selected material from an Asian, Caucasian, Hispanic, and African American. Perhaps they wished to forestall criticism that they were presenting the genome of just one of these social racial groups, that is, perhaps they were varying the nonexistent effects of what they themselves knew had no causes. Or, perhaps they wanted to include as much genetic variety in their samples as possible, because, variety, after all, is biologically real. Even though the distribution of variation in the human species does not support a racial taxonomy and most variety occurs locally (within what are called the same races), including members of all social races would maximize variety in the sample of the human species by attempting to include that 6 to 10 percent of the 0.2 percent of genetic material in which humans vary, which does seem to correspond to social racial difference. But in that case, I cannot help but wonder whether the genome donors were "typical" members of their respective social racial groups, and if so, how that decision was made.

5.

Genealogy
and Ideas of Race

The Concept of Genealogy

Folk ideas of race are related to an assumption that individuals inherit their racial identities from parents and ancestors. As explained in chapter 4, heredity takes place via specific genes that retain their integrity and identity over generations. That is, there is no blending or mixing of genes from one generation to the next. The genomes, or totalities of genes, belonging to parents contain all the possibilities of the genes that their children can inherit. That grounds the folk sense in which children resemble their parents as a general biological principle. But not all of the genes of both parents can be inherited by their offspring, and there is no certainty that a child will resemble a parent in phenotypes that express dominant genes. Strictly speaking, children do not inherit traits or phenotypes from parents, but genes, which along with internal and external environmental influences and developmental factors have the potential to determine traits or phenotypes.

There is nothing about "racial traits" that makes them racial in genetic terms. Physical traits that society deems racial are heritable, but their underlying genes are merely parts—no different in principle from other parts—of the human genome in its allelic variety, and are therefore subject to the regularities of Mendelian heredity shared by all alleles. Therefore, there is no certainty that a child will inherit those traits possessed by parents, which society considers to be racial.

Parents have children who are the same race they are, as the result of the history of our species, and its cultures. Over the history of the species, human beings have chosen mates who are geographically close. So-called racial traits are recent adaptations within groups to immediate environmental conditions. Since the environment usually changes in ways that are continuous geographically, the so-called racial traits of indigenous populations or groups that have lived in particular places for relatively long time periods have been called *clines*.[1] Still, racial traits are by no means perfect clines today, because modern humans have been extremely mobile. The cultural cause of the resemblance between children and parents in racial traits is the tradition, within societies divided into hierarchical racial taxonomies, that people choose mates of the same race. As causes of the resemblance of children to parents in racial traits, species history and cultural tradition have the same restrictions: Assuming that relevant environmental and developmental factors are constant, we may conclude this. Phenetically and genetically, children resemble both their parents in so-called racial traits if, phenetically and genetically, their parents resemble each other in those traits. Genetic differences between parents in racial traits can result in phenetic and genetic differences in children from either or both parents, as well as from siblings who have the same parents.

It is important to remember that the subject of genealogy is different from the subject of transmission genetics. The subject of transmission genetics is genes, either singly or in chromosomes or genomes. The subject of genealogy is relations of whole individuals, either singly or in groups. These two subjects are often conflated in folk discourse, for instance, when we say that an individual has her mother's eye shape or his father's hair color. Individuals are indeed descended from other individuals, and it is informative and interesting to construct family genealogies. But the phenotypes for specific traits of individuals are not necessarily the same as their underlying genotypes or the same as the phenotypes or genotypes of their parents and ancestors for the same kinds of traits. And, the phenotypes of any one individual are no more their parents' than their own—their parents transmit the genes underlying them, but the genes are copied fresh in each generation, and genes and phenetic traits belong as much to an individual as they do to his or her parents.

The confusion about genealogy and transmission genetics increases with those biological traits deemed racial. Consider, for example, the American assumption that a person *must* be black if she has a black ancestor. This "one-drop" rule not only falsely assumes the existence of a dominant "black gene," which is racially defining, but it associates that gene with generational heredity, so that the "black gene" is defining of the entire individual. Only those genes that as combinations are present in every member of a species or higher taxon could qualify as both genetically transmitted and generational in that way. For instance, *Homo sapiens*, as a species, share genes that are defining of the species, and every *Homo sapiens* must have *Homo sapiens* parents, and if he or she reproduces, must have *Homo sapiens* children. There is no evidence that genetic racial differences are of the same qualitative magnitude as genetic species differences.

In principle, the essentialist theme in folk ideas of racial heredity *could not* have a scientific basis, for two reasons. First, there is no evidence that general racial essences exist. Second, the apparently racial genes that in combination could make up racial essences are not inherited together, and it is not the case that all members of distinct social races have the same racial phenotypes. And yet, apart from beliefs about the heredity of racial essences or racial traits in combination, folk notions of racial heredity may look as though they could be scientifically grounded if they were conceptualized in one or more of these three genealogical ways: races are *clades*; races are families; individual racial identity derives from family racial identity. In this chapter, I will examine these three genealogical candidates for a scientific basis of race.

Races as Clades

Cladistics is the school of biological taxonomy originated by Willi Hennig in 1950.[2] By the time Hennig wrote, evolutionary taxonomists had succeeded in showing that, in accord with Darwin's principle, most recognized animal taxa above the species level were *monophyletic*. A monophyletic taxon is "exclusively composed of descendants of a common ancestor."[3] Hennig was the author of the principle that lines of descent "split" at points where uniquely derived hereditary traits first occur. A clade is thus a multi-generational group (that is, all of its members do not exist at the same time) with a trait that comes after a split in a line of descent. A clade itself may in turn split into further generational groups after other distinct derived traits occur, and it would thus give rise to further clades. As Ernst Mayr explains it, cladistic analysis is a highly useful taxonomic tool, in theory, because it enables both the reconstruction of genealogy and the nonarbitrary classification of individuals into taxa. But, Mayr points out that, as Darwin insisted, genealogy alone may not be sufficient for classification. This is because adaptive evolutionary changes may result in differences among groups within the same clade or branch. For example, crocodiles and birds could be located within the same clade and so could chimpanzees and human beings. But, those solely cladistic classifications would ignore important evolutionary divisions.[4]

Still, for some today, the cladistic concept has appeal as a possible scientific basis of race. Robin Andreasen suggests that the lack of biological similarity within social racial groups need not preclude a scientific foundation of race, if races are viewed as clades. Andreasen proposes that the genealogical tracking of human migratory groups, which can be derived from the mitochondrial DNA comparisons developed by Luigi Cavalli-Sforza and his colleagues, supports a system of racial genealogical branching over the history of *Homo sapiens*. In her view, the major human mt DNA groups that, based on distinctive mutations, can be identified as having split from each other, after having first split from an original African population, are clades; descendants of the original African population that remained in Africa also form a clade, and descendants who left after the first migration also form a clade. Based on independent archaeological evidence for human migrations, Cavalli-Sforza's mt DNA branching was also mapped onto the continental locations of the indigenous or long-dwelling populations from whom the original mt DNA samples were collected. This branching appeals to Andreasen as a cladistic expression of race, because common sense race is associated with beliefs about the geographical locations of ancestral racial groups (Africa, Asia, Europe, the Americas).[5] Andreasen's cladistic genealogical model of race would also apparently preserve common sense intuitions that there is a greater racial difference between blacks and all other groups than between any other two racial groups, because it is supposed to be derived from the mt DNA mutational data that supports a greater division between the African group and all others than between any other two groups. But the mt DNA mutational data is not presented or commonly interpreted as a foundation for common sense racial intuitions. So there is something wrong here.

Andreasen's proposal works as an independent scientific basis for social racial taxonomy only if its dependence on social racial taxonomy is ignored. Members of social races do share the derived traits of specific mt DNA mutations that could qualify them as monophyletic groups in the cladistic sense. This is to say that they are genealogical in a distinctive way. However, as noted earlier in chapter 2, mt DNA is not protein coding and is therefore causally unrelated to anything that could be considered a racial trait in common sense. It could be countered that the mt DNA mutations link the recognized social groups to geographical areas and that the geographical areas are empirically associated with distinctive common sense racial traits, because of environmental adaptations such as the dark skin shade of the African population. But this requires assumptions that only Africans have dark skin and that skin shade differences are as discontinuous as genealogical mt DNA mutations. At this point, we need to remember that skin shades are clines. Indeed, Nina Jablonski and George Chaplin have recently presented evidence that skin color variations are related to the regulation of ultraviolet radiation in correlation with latitude. They believe that ancient hominids had unpigmented skin covered with dark hair and that first dark skin and then light skin evolved. They conclude that "skin coloration in humans is adaptive and labile."[6] If Jablonski and Chaplin are correct, then there is no empirical evidence for the correlation of specific skin colors with specific mt DNA mutational lineages, even though the latter might be correlated with geographical locations over past millennia. In other words, whether at any time in the past the inhabitants of any of the racially identified continents had the racial traits we now associate with inhabitants of that continent is an open empirical question that is not determined by connections between mt DNA mutations and geographical locations.

There are two other obvious problems with the races-as-clades notion. A clade consists of descendants of a common ancestor with a distinctive derived trait, whereas a race in the social sense may contain members who are descendants of other races. More serious conceptually, cladistics as a taxonomic methodology has always been applied to taxa at the species level or higher.[7] If cladistics were applied to the subspecies level, there would have to be independent evidence that the subspecies groups were already well-delineated according to some other biological classificatory system such as phenetics. Without independent justification for an application of cladistics to groups more specific than species—justification that would have to be something other than common sense notions of race, which are themselves in need of biological justification—there would be nothing to stop the application of cladistics to very small genealogical groups with distinct hereditary traits, such as families. The problem with applying cladistics that far down is that it fails to preserve the taxonomic feature of cladism, which relates to distinctive attributes of groups that are otherwise recognizable as evolutionary units. On the other hand, insofar as cladism does not rely on phenetic classification at all, there is in principle no reason why clades cannot be relatively small generational groups within species. But, if cladism is extended this way, then to call races "clades" is no more informative than calling them familial lines of descent or generational populations. And the vacuity of capturing races with such a cladistic application would also hold for other generational groups thus captured. As a result, the label 'clade' would add no new scientific information to the common sense knowledge that human beings have genealogies.

If cladism cannot be informatively extended below the species level, then it is only metaphorical to call races clades. While metaphor may be useful within science, the metaphoric use of a scientific term in a nonscientific context does not provide a scientific basis for that context. Also problematic is the fact that those unfamiliar with the science on which the metaphor depends may think that the metaphoric usage is a literal one and conclude that the nonscientific context has been given a scientific foundation when it has not. To say that races are clades in this metaphoric way, may thus appear, to the scientifically innocent, to certify that there is a scientific basis for race.

Races as Families

There is a presumption in folk racial discourse that members of the same race are more closely related to each other than to members of different races. Such presumed shared kinship among members of the same race, who are not otherwise known to be familial relatives, is generally believed to be a valid reason for loyalty and altruistic obligations to same-race members, which would not be extended to members of different races. Moral discussion concerning out-marriage, observance of traditional cultural practices, and benefit to one's race, generally seem to be based on this presumption of race kinship, albeit in ways that are often vague. Some liberatory scholars dismiss kinship-type moral ties to same-race members, as backward, essentialist remnants of tribalism, which are oppressive and degrading to individuals. These issues support considerable contemporary scholarly debate.[8] It is toward this academic context, and not so much popular opinion, that the question of whether there is a scientific foundation for the notion of races as families, should be addressed. In the discussion, there would be a shift from a physical scientific basis to a social science basis, a shift to history, sociology, or more broadly, social theory.

The general question for social science is whether and how a family notion of race could avoid false physical science assumptions about race. A mistaken answer lies in W. E. B. Du Bois's 1897 address to the American Negro Academy, "The Conservation of Races."[9] Du Bois disagreed with the current scientific view of race. He cited the inadequacy of anthropometric data to define racial groups and disagreed with the consensus that there were three major races.[10] Du Bois thought that there were eight major races: the Slavs of eastern Europe, the Teutons of middle Europe, the English of Great Britain and America, the Romance nations of southern and western Europe, the Negroes of Africa and America, the Semitic people of western Asia and northern Africa, the Hindus of central Asia, and the Mongolians of eastern Asia.[11] Overall, Du Bois's difference with the late-nineteenth-century scientists of race was not the later objection that their belief in the existence of races was not justified by the empirical data, but his intuition that there was more to racial taxonomy and racial identity than the physical sciences revealed. Thus, he claimed that races, "while they perhaps transcend scientific definition, nevertheless, are clearly defined to the eye of the Historian and Sociologist." Du Bois believed that world history was the history of races, and he answered his rhetorical question, "What, then is a race?" with a definition of a race as a family:

> It is a vast family of human beings, generally of common blood and language, always of common history, traditions and impulses, which are both voluntarily and involuntarily striving together for the accomplishment of certain more or less vividly conceived ideals of life.[12]

In the 1990s K. Anthony Appiah challenged Du Bois's notion of common history as a way of defining race on the grounds that groups need to be identified independently of history, or past events experienced by the members at different times, before it can be asserted that the members of those groups have the same history.[13] Appiah interprets Du Bois as relying on the now-falsified nineteenth-century scientific ideas of race, which he claims to be transcending, in order to identify races in the first place.[14] Du Bois's unquestioning use of the term 'blood' in conjunction with race, throughout the 1897 paper, in itself supports Appiah's charge, because it presupposes a physical racial essentialism.[15] Appiah's critique, however, centers on the essentialism in the link between biology and culture in Du Bois's concept of race.[16] Appiah points out that the notion of geographical place seems to underlie Du Bois's taxonomy of eight races, and he asserts that what Du Bois should have been talking about was not "races," or groups defined by false biology, but civilizations, or groups defined by "intention and meaning."[17]

One problem with Appiah's critique of Du Bois's use of false scientific notions of race is that he doesn't clearly explain why, given the knowledge of the lack of a scientific basis for race, it remains lucid to talk about the history and sociology of groups that are identified by the false biological concepts. For example, it is now broadly understood that the American designation of February as "Black History Month" is meant to recognize distinctive aspects of the history of African Americans, which would otherwise be ignored. Even though those people identified by others and themselves as African Americans are not a race in a sense that has the bases in science that racial taxonomy is assumed to have, this group does have a history. Of course, Appiah would not deny that. But the point Appiah neglects is that their shared history does partly constitute their identity, insofar as that identity is chosen and constructed by African Americans. And here, there is a turn in the meaning of identity, from objective taxonomic identification to intentions and meanings. Not incidentally, intentions and meanings are what would ground any social science theory of race, because it is the beliefs about race, false or not, and the behavior associated with them, which form the subject of the social science in question. (I will say more about this in chapter 7.)

The problem with Du Bois's definition of race was not that he used biological notions of race to provide the ontology of a "transcendent" sociohistorical notion, although that is a problem insofar as the biology was false and/or insofar as "transcendent" suggests a construction that is not physical. Rather, the problem for us now was that Du Bois wanted to conserve what we know to be false biological race, so that the black race could develop and express its unique racial potential:

> We are Negroes, members of a vast historic race that from the very dawn of creation has slept, but half awakening in the dark forests of its African fatherland. We are the first fruits of this new nation, the harbinger of that black to-morrow which is yet destined to soften the whiteness of the Teutonic to-day. We are that people whose subtle sense of song has given America its only American music, its only American fairy tales, its only touch of pathos and humor amid its mad money-getting plutocracy. As such, it is our duty to conserve our physical powers, our intellectual endowments, our spiritual ideas; as a race we must strive by race organizations, by race solidarity, by race unity to the realization of that broader humanity which freely recognizes differences in men, but sternly deprecates inequality in their opportunities of development.[18]

Thus, Du Bois was thinking within the original Humean-Kantian essentialist notion of racial taxonomy (see chapter 1), but he wanted an opportunity to prove that blacks were not inferior to whites within that taxonomy. So, how to complete Appiah's critique of Du Bois? The social histories of racial groups, the lack of a biological foundation for racial groups, and the failure of biology to define social races—these things need to be related to each other in a way that is crystal clear on a conceptual level capable of considering them all. Only that could reconcile social science studies of race with the present biological knowledge. Philosophically, the solution is simple. Sociologists and historians who reject false biological taxonomies of race need to *mention* those taxonomies in describing the groups of human beings delineated by them, but they ought not to accept those taxonomies in their own first order ontology; they ought not themselves to *use* the taxonomies.

Consider the contrast between the history of farmers and the history of witches, or a contemporary study of these groups today. For both witches and farmers, the social scientist will investigate behavior that is mediated by human beliefs. Within farming communities and the wider society, farmers are believed to have those skills that identify them as farmers. That is, farmers are believed to exist as an occupational category of human beings, and that belief is shared by empiricist social scientists. Within occult communities and in parts of the wider society, witches are believed to have skills that identify them as witches. Other members of the broader society and empiricist social scientists accept the existence of human beings who are believed to be witches and the existence of the beliefs about the skills of witches, but they do not themselves accept that there are people who have skills that identify them as witches. The fact that witches can be grammatical subjects of meaningful sentences does not entail that witches exist in the way they and their cohorts believe they exist. Social scientists should mention and use the term 'farmer,' but they should mention but not use the term 'witch.' Race in the biological sense, and any of its specificities (such as black, white, Asian, and so forth) is like 'witch.' It should be mentioned but not used. In the words of social theory, it is always *emic*, and never *etic*, and Peter Lopston's explanation of this distinction deserves detailed attention:

> A description or perspective is emic when it represents a piece of behavior or other human reality in terms that would be recognized and endorsed by the human beings involved in that behavior or reality. An emic account, then, will be meant to correspond to an agent's point of view, and to make sense from that agent's perspective (or "phenomenological stance"). A description or perspective is etic when it represents a piece of behavior or other human reality from the stance of an external observer, especially an observer aiming to produce an accurate theoretical account, which may or may not correspond to or utilize the terminology or conceptual categories of the agent. The emic then is participant-relative, and the etic observer-relative. Emic and etic *can* coincide (that is, be identical), though typically they will not. There may be corresponding emic and etic descriptions or explanations of the same

event or phenomenon, in which case both may be literally true or accurate, or just one may be, or neither. Or one of the perspectives may pick out or express something that the other one fails to.[19]

An understanding of the emic-etic distinction ought to inform social science description and cultural criticism of race, regardless of whether it is convenient to actually use quotation marks. Where emic and etic ontologies do not coincide, it is still possible to undertake both emic and etic description and analysis at the same time, when the emic perspective expresses a liberatory ideal shared on the etic level. Thus, Appiah clearly has great respect for Du Bois as a cultural thinker, even though Du Bois's subscription of false nineteenth-century racial ontology renders his beliefs emic for Appiah:

> In his early work, Du Bois took race for granted and sought to revalue one pole of the opposition of white black. The received concept is a hierarchy, a vertical structure, and Du Bois wished to rotate the axis, to give race a "horizontal" reading. Challenge the assumption that there can be an axis, however oriented in the space of values, and the project fails for loss of presuppositions. In his later work, Du Bois—whose life's work was, in a sense, an attempt at just this impossible project—was unable to escape the notion of race he had explicitly rejected. We may borrow his own metaphor: though he saw the dawn coming, he never faced the sun. And we must surely admit that he was followed in this by many in our culture today; we too live in the dusk of that dawn.[20]

When, as Appiah suggests, civilizations, instead of races, become the subject of inquiry, much that is believed to be true of races may not be translated into the first order subjects, predicates, and sentences of the inquiry. This is not surprising, because the scholar of civilizations, cultures, and subcultures directly addresses a real and taxonomically unwieldy domain. A study of these entities with a reserved option to either use or mention the subjects and predicates found in discourse within them is not a "transcendence" of the physical bases of these entities, but a different kind of science than the science of physical realities. If any subject within a civilization does not have the physical basis that can be studied in a relevant physical science, then even though the subject is believed to have such a physical base within the civilization, the social scientist cannot suspend disbelief in the course of inquiry. Race and witchcraft are not the only subjects in this category. They are joined by Santa Claus and varied deities.

Let's return now to the notion of races-as-families as a subject in biological science. What are believed to be races in common sense are often generations of descendants of a founding population that occupied a specific geographical place such as Africa, parts of Asia, or the Americas. During the time period when these populations bred within themselves, they were distinct populations, with members having more and closer ties of kinship with co-members, than with members of other populations. Such populations were, in effect, very large human families. Wherever such isolated multigenerational populations exist now and in the recent past, they would also be very large families. Such populations are real and their genealogy can, where records exist, be reconstructed and studied. But can they provide a scientific basis for a genealogical concept of a race as a very large family?

If racial categories are understood to be small in number, say less than 50, then the genealogies of actual populations cannot ground the concept of race. Actual populations are subject to change, based both on new people joining them and descendants leaving, so whatever racial traits are associated with them are going to be highly variable. Furthermore, given the facts of human microevolution, there are likely thousands if not hundreds of thousands of such populations over human history.[21] It is informative in terms of genealogy, population genetics, and transmission genetics to say that an individual is a member of a given ongoing isolated population. However, it is not informative in terms of population genetics or transmission genetics to identify an individual based on ancestry in such a population if that individual also has other ancestry or is not presently part of the isolated breeding population in question. Thus, to call people "African Americans" on the grounds that some of their ancestors were part of an isolated breeding population (of which there would have been many) existing in the past in Africa is not informative in scientific terms. Given these considerations, the genealogical notion of races-as-families is not a viable scientific basis for common sense ideas of race. (Although, the study of isolated populations as large families remains informative in its own right.)

Families as a Source of Racial Identity

The American one-drop rule of black identity has been applied in the context of a close relationship between family racial identity and individual racial identity. American families are usually considered to have monoracial identities that their individual members "inherit" in a mythical way that includes cultural and physical inheritance.[22] In a society where white racial identity means that there are no nonwhite ancestors, white family identity has been protected by restricting the marriage of whites to whites. While nonwhites have been less concerned with their own "racial purity" than whites, they have still been reluctant to approve of racial intermarriage, for several reasons: demographic loss to the nonwhite community of the out-marrying spouse and subsequent offspring; the symbolic power of out-marriage to suggest that available nonwhite mates are inferior; lapses in carrying on cultural traditions associated with the nonwhite community.[23] All of these attitudes and practices raise the question of whether the racial identity of families is in fact a basis of the racial identity of individuals. A negative answer is easily derived from conclusions already drawn in this chapter and chapter 4: If the realities of transmission genetics and biological heredity do not ground common sense racial taxonomies, then, a fortiori, the social arrangements associated with distorted understandings of those realities cannot do so. If parents resemble each other phenotypically in those traits deemed racial, then their children may resemble them. But, the phenotypical *racial* resemblance in this case depends on biological criteria for both race and racial resemblance, which refer to things presumed to exist outside of the biological facts of family heredity. Those things are "races," abstract categories that are used as mediating terms in racial descriptions of family inheritance, as in "John is black because his father is black." Therefore, family inheritance alone cannot be a basis for racial identity.

Even if there were empirically justified criteria for racial identity and racial resemblance, and the breeding pairs within each race always shared them, social families could still not ground racial identity, because social families are not the same things as biological families. If the racial criteria and races existed, then biological families could be the source of individual racial identities, but only if social families were always exactly the same as biological families.

The case of Thomas Jefferson's nonwhite putative descendants is a striking example of the discrepancy between biological and social families, which has always been silently assumed in American history. A few commonly agreed upon facts drive the recurrent interest in the Jefferson story: DNA analysis can sometimes positively identify genealogical relations and other times rule them out; individuals of different social races can interbreed and produce fertile offspring; it was common practice among American slave owners to have sexual relations with female slaves, resulting in children who were considered racially black and almost never accepted as family members by their white biological kin.[24]

Jefferson inherited the slave Sally Hemmings as part of his late wife's estate. Sally and Jefferson's wife had the same white father, although Sally's mother was a Negro slave. During his lifetime, Jefferson was rumored to have fathered at least two of Sally Hemmings's six children, and the rumor persisted throughout American history, although Jefferson's official (white) descendants, that is, his social family, denied it. Historians traditionally supported the belief of the descendants of Thomas Jefferson's daughter Martha Jefferson Randolph that Sally Hemmings's youngest son, Eston (born in 1808), resembled Thomas Jefferson because his father was either Samuel or Peter Carr, who were sons of Jefferson's sister. In other words, the explanation for the resemblance between Thomas and Eston was that Eston was Thomas's great-nephew and that they both resembled Thomas's father, who would have been Eston's maternal great-grandfather.

In 1998, Eugene Foster and colleagues compared Y-chromosome DNA haplotypes from male line descendants of Field Jefferson, a paternal uncle of Thomas Jefferson's—Thomas Jefferson himself had no acknowledged existing male descendants—with male-line descendants of Sally Hemmings's first son, Thomas Woodson, and her last son, Eston Hemmings Jefferson. There was a distinctive, rare haplotype present only in males in Thomas Jefferson's family, which had not been found in European males outside of that family. The results of the DNA comparisons led the researchers to conclude that Jefferson fathered Eston but not Thomas Woodson. They could not rule out the possibility that one of Thomas Jefferson's nephews had fathered Eston, but in the absence of historical evidence for this claim, they discounted it.[25] But, regardless of whether Thomas Jefferson or another member of his paternal line of descent was Eston's father, the point for our purposes is that someone in the Jefferson paternal family had to have been a male ancestor of Eston's, because of the unique Y-chromosomal marker in that male line.[26]

John Jefferson of Illinois, the direct descendant of Sally Hemmings who was a donor from the Hemmings line for the DNA comparison, was descended from a family that had traditionally denied their relation to Thomas Jefferson, precisely because it came through Sally Hemmings's descendants, and the Hemmings of Illinois had always identified as racially white. Their ancestor, Eston Hemmings Jefferson, had been able to pass for white and his descendants were able to socially shed their Hemmings ancestry.[27] Thus, a contemporary white American family, in acknowledging black ancestry, has been able to graphically illustrate the ongoing difference between biological and social family genealogy. As a result, another white American family—the socially recognized descendants of Thomas Jefferson in Virginia—have become obligated to concede that they are not a purely white family.[28] We can see from this that although social race is distinct from biological race, because social race as an emic social concept contains the assumption that race is biological, proven biological kin are automatically presumed to be proven social kin, and vice versa. The long-standing resistance among Jefferson's officially white descendants to acknowledging nonwhite biological relatives can be understood as part of a mechanism protecting the presumed biological whiteness of white social families. Running through the Jefferson-Hemmings story, right up to newspaper reports in 2001, is the assumption that Sally Hemmings was black even though her father was white. This application of the one-drop rule continues through the assumption that Eston Hemmings Jefferson, who was known as E. H. Jefferson after he assimilated into white society in Wisconsin, was black, and that his great-great grandson John Jefferson and his siblings and their descendants are also black.[29] It is ironic that it was DNA from a member of a white-identified family that ultimately confirmed the existence of Thomas Jefferson's "black" descendants. However, the acceptance of the DNA analysis in this case further attests to a very broad understanding that DNA is not an indicator of racial identity, even though it is highly useful for determining biological family genealogy.

The location of family records and addresses of putative kin through the Internet and the availability of almost do-it-yourself DNA analysis kits now make it quite easy for individuals to reconstruct their family genealogies.[30] Racial identity will continue to motivate such searches as will interest in the attainments and status of ancestors that include racial identity. For instance, many African Americans would like to know exactly where in Africa their ancestors lived before slavery.[31] (And African Americans as well as white Americans are pleased to discover ancestors of high social status.) But, it should be noted that questions about ancestry are specific or particular, for example, Was Eston the son of Thomas?, while questions about race are abstract, for example, Is the Jefferson family (either the midwestern or southern branch) white? We are left with the vacuous truth that human beings are descended from other human beings, each with distinctive biological and social characteristics, and with the conclusion that given what we now know about biology, racial identity is never more than an emic characteristic.

However, another irony about the association of racial identity with family identity emerges as a result of contemporary realities of families in which biological parents belong to different social races. Interracial marriage has been legal throughout the United States only since 1967.[32] Before then, the majority of mixed black and white Americans were illegitimate. Their ancestry represented shame within nonwhite communities, because of their illegitimacy, and unacceptable stigma among whites as a result of racism. Black-white "mixtures" were not the sole combination, because there were white-Indian and black-Indian offspring since colonial days, and after immigration, white-Asian and black-Asian, as well as varied combinations among all of the racial groups.[33]

The U.S. census has had a varied history in presenting racial options for self-identification to Americans, and until the census of 2000, it was acceptable to check only one box for racial identification.[34] Most writers estimate that from 1967 until the late 1990s, the number of births in interracial marriages grew from 500,000 to two million.[35] The result of the 2000 census opportunity to check more than one box was that seven million Americans identified as "multiracial." This group, reported as containing 5 percent of blacks, 6 percent of Hispanics, 14 percent of Asians, and 2.3 percent of whites, was characterized in an early interpretation of the data as "a small largely youthful generation."[36] If we can assume that the multiracial identification was based on respondents' knowledge that their parents were members of the different races they checked, and that the respondents and their parents considered themselves members of the same family, then here is an instance in which social family identity is erasing the discrepancy between itself and biological family identity, insofar as race is a factor. This is ironic, because in the United States the discrepancy between the two types of family identity was established to protect monoracial social families, in a way that seemed biological. Of course, the apparent biological basis of family racial identity persists. For instance, as of this writing, in Albany, New York, during the spring of 2001, a local cell phone company offers a plan that includes four phones for family members. The plan is advertised in a television commercial that is presented as comical, because it depicts groups of individuals with different racial appearances attempting to apply for the plan as families. Nevertheless, the multiracial respondents to the 2000 census have shown that not everyone believes that families need to be monoracial.

Race and Contemporary Anthropology

Disciplinary Connections

Most twentieth-century philosophers writing about race focused on social identities and racism. This is understandable in that philosophy is a field in the humanities. Anthropologists, by contrast, have steadily focused on the biological aspects of race, revising over the twentieth century what their predecessors constructed during the nineteenth. Although the founders of the modern sciences, including anthropology, started out as philosophers, philosophy of science is a relatively new specialization in the field of philosophy, and its model has largely been the science of physics. Thus, philosophy of biology is new, as are philosophies of the social sciences. I am not aware that philosophy of anthropology is a recognized specialization in philosophy of science, but I believe that there is a very important area of inquiry in which philosophical analysis of biological ideas of race intersects with theoretical analysis of biological race in anthropology.

As the underlying biological information relative to race has become available, anthropologists have not hesitated to discard earlier essentialist taxonomies of human variety. Indeed, anthropologists now substantially agree that there is no biological foundation for the historical notions of human racial divisions. However, I think that there is a distinctively philosophical contribution that can be made to the anthropological consensus, and I will try to establish that in this chapter.

Let me begin with a summary of the previous chapters, here. In chapter 1, I showed how Hume and Kant assumed without empirical justification that there were natural human distinctions underlying social racial taxonomy. Implicitly or explicitly, they were both commited to racial essences. These racial essences were for a long time believed to cause differences in psychology, talents, and culture. The existence of biological racial essences and the links between those essences and other aspects of human life were two distinct versions of racial essentialism. In chapter 2, I explored the history of the belief that world geographical differences are an empirical basis for race. Given studies in contemporary population genetics, I concluded that geographical location has no causal bearing on social racial taxonomy, for two reasons: the environmental adaptations associated with geography are continuous, while racial divisions are discrete; the evidence for geographical ancestral origin in populations, namely persistent mutations in mitochondrial DNA, is unrelated to social physical racial characteristics. Chapter 3 addressed the possibility of a phenotypical basic for social race, with a focus on human skin shade, and blood-type variations. Skin shade varies continuously, without any qualitative differences that correspond to social racial differences, and membership in blood-type groups varies independently of other recognized racial traits. Chapter 4 was a brief excursion into transmission genetics, post-Mendel. The possibility of hereditary, general race factors was excluded, because the independent inheritance of genes that cause specific racial traits precludes it. No social racial group has a distinctive set of so-called racial traits, which is shared by each one of its members. Neither does a population basis for racial taxonomy work. A substitution of populations with distinct proportions of inherited phenotypes, for races can not take place without presupposing the social identification of races, which is itself in need of an independent scientific justification. In chapter 5, it became evident that cladistic and family-type genealogies can ground social racial taxonomies only if such taxonomies, which, again, are themselves in need of justification, are presupposed and projected onto the genealogies. Essences, geography, phenotypes, genotypes, and genealogy are the only known candidates for physical scientific bases of race. Each fails. Therefore, there is no physical scientific basis for social racial taxonomy. Returning to my proviso in the Introduction, if common sense racial taxonomy is assumed to be real *because* it has a basis in science, and it does not have a basis in science, then common sense race is unreal. The latter is a philosophical, or logical, point.

As stated, there is a consensus in anthropology that race is unreal. Still, I think that the presentation of the anthropological consensus about race would be stronger if it were made clear what is meant by "race." Therefore, in this chapter, I want to consider several theoretical aspects of the 1998 American Anthropological Association Statement on "Race" and the commentary on an earlier draft of this statement, published in the *Anthropology Newsletter* (*AN*) between September 1997 and September 1998. I hope to show how the nonexistence of race, that is, the falsity of biological racial essentialism, makes it unnecessary to argue against links between racial biology and culture, that is, cultural racial essentialism. Given that human variety is real but not racial, it should also be possible to understand how limited forensic classification or typology may be pursued without racialist—much less racist—projections. As well, agreement about the nonexistence of race has important implications for public health policy and medical practice (and for speculations about connections between race and IQ, which I will address in the next chapter).

Logical Implications of the Nonexistence of Race

The 1998 AAA Statement on "Race" is a work of anthropological theory because it interprets past empirical research and, where accepted, would influence future research. At the same time, the statement is meant to present the facts about race "to the public" in a way that will increase social justice.[1] Late-nineteenth and early-twentieth-century scientists were insistent about imposing a socially constructed hierarchical taxonomy of biological race on the public, partly as a justification for slavery and segregation.[2] Middle- and late-twentieth-century anthropologists were generally less firm about disabusing the public about false notions of biological race. The 1998 AAA statement forthrightly asserts to the public that human biological races do not exist, and it is, on those grounds, a pivotal historical document. Furthermore, discussion in *AN* prior to the final draft of the statement made it clear that "the public" was meant to include politicians, teachers, and scholars in other fields, who for one reason or another are extremely resistant to the idea that race as they imagine it is nonexistent.[3] Let us now consider the first part of the text of the 1998 AAA Statement on "Race":

> In the US both scholars and the general public have been conditioned to viewing human races as natural and separate divisions within the human species based on visible physical differences. With the vast expansion of scientific knowledge in this century, however, it has become clear that human populations are not unambiguous, clearly demarcated, biologically distinct groups. Evidence from the analysis of genetics (e.g., DNA) indicates that there is greater variation within racial groups than between them. This means that most physical variation, about 94% lies *within* so-called racial groups. Conventional geographic racial groupings differ from one another only in about 6% of their genes. In neighboring populations there is much over-lapping of genes and their phenotypic (physical) expressions. Throughout history whenever different groups have come into contact, they have interbred. The continued sharing of genetic materials has maintained all of humankind as a single species.... Today scholars in many fields argue that race as it is understood in the USA was a social mechanism invented during the 18th century to refer to those populations brought together in colonial America: the English and other European settlers, the conquered Indian people, and those peoples of Africa brought in to provide slave labor.[4]

It should be noted as a factual clarification to the statement that since it is 94 percent of the human genetic difference overall that falls within races, and that overall difference is 0.2 percent, the 6 percent of genetic difference resulting from perceived racial difference is 6 percent of 0.2 percent of all human genetic material, which is 0.012 percent, or less than 1/8000.[5] And, as Jonathan Marks points out, the difference based on racial difference as defined by social categories may be even less. The figures used for the difference in the statement are based on differences in mitochondrial DNA, which occur about five times more rapidly than nuclear genetic differences in the histories of species. Marks therefore suggests that the amount of nuclear genetic difference based on preselected social racial categories is probably 0.0024 percent or less than 1/40,000 of human genetic material.[6]

Following the claim in the 1998 statement about the nonexistence of biological race is an explanation of how hierarchical theories of racial difference functioned historically to justify cultural domination by whites of indigenous people, colonized people, Africans, and Jews. The statement closes with the broad anthropological tenet that human cultural behavior is learned and all normal human beings are able to learn any culture. Furthermore, studies of infant and childhood learning confirm the effect of culture on human identities. Therefore, it is concluded:

> that present-day inequalities between so-called racial groups are not consequences of their biological inheritance but products of historical and contemporary social, economic, educational, and political circumstances.[7]

In 1952, Claude Lévi-Strauss wrote an essay that explained how cultural differences among human beings were not the result of biological or racial differences, but of history and environment.[8] During the 1950s and 1960s, this position was developed in different ways by L. C. Dunn, Michel Leiris, and others. The consensus within this group about the independence of culture and human aptitude, from biology and race, was expressed in four statements on *racism*, or discrimination and beliefs about the inferiority and superiority of different races, which were first published by UNESCO.[9] Throughout these statements, the existence of biological race is not clearly and directly contested. The liberatory force of the UNESCO statements lies in the proclamation that human cultural achievement is not determined or constrained by biological racial identity:

> The peoples of the world today appear to possess equal biological potentialities for attaining any civilizational level. Differences in the achievements of different peoples must be attributed solely to their cultural history.[10]

We have seen that the 1998 AAA Statement on "Race" begins with the claim that biological race does not exist. It is traditional for scientists to base their claims about the existence or nonexistence of things on empirical data. But empirical data may confirm or disconfirm the existence of things on different levels of generality. Human biological racial taxonomy, or *race*, is a very general construct. The lack of empirical referents for the construct of racial taxonomy (that is, for 'race') precludes the existence of more specific aspects of such a taxonomy, and of the interaction of elements of such a taxonomy with things that do exist. This is simply a matter of logic. The

1998 AAA Statement on "Race" would have been theoretically stronger, as well as potentially more enlightening for the public, if some of the logical truths concerning racial taxonomy were clearly stated. The relevant logical truths follow from two assumptions: nonexistent entities cannot be causes, effects, or objects in relationships with things that do exist; nonexistent entities cannot have subcategories that exist. Thus, for example, unicorns, which do not exist, cannot have an impact on existing ecological systems, and since unicorns do not exist as a general category, it is impossible for gray or golden unicorns to exist. The relevant logical truths about race are as follow:

1. If there is no human biological racial taxonomy, then there is no human biological racial hierarchy.
2. If there is no human biological racial taxonomy, then there are no specific biological races.
3. If there are no biological races, then there are no pure or mixed biological races.
4. If there is no human biological racial taxonomy, then there are no biological causal connections between biological race and culture or psychology.
5. If there is no human biological racial taxonomy, then there are no biological causal connections between biological race and other aspects of human biology.
6. If there is no human biological racial taxonomy, then there are no biological causal connections between race and ethnicity.[11]

To say that items 1 through 6 are logically true is another way of saying that they are a priori true. They need no further empirical confirmation, and they are immune to further empirical findings. If the first clauses in 1 through 6 are true, that is, if race does not exist, then there is no scientific finding that could lend credence to links between race and hierarchy, purity, culture, biology, or ethnicity. However, the 1998 AAA Statement on "Race" implies that both the nonexistence of race and the ineffectiveness of racial difference for causing cultural difference have been empirically confirmed. But, as noted, if race does not exist, it is logically impossible that race biologically causes culture, so the facts concerning the universality of human learning, and the ways in which culture determines identities, are beside the point. That these facts are reiterated almost fifty years after Lévi-Strauss and his cohort brought international attention to them suggests that the authors of the AAA statement take them to be confirmation of the nonexistence of race. This in turn implies that if the facts in question were otherwise, race might have the biological reality it is now falsely assumed to have by the public. But, the evidence for the nonexistence of race, or the lack of evidence for the existence of race, has to be independent of 'nature vs. nurture' interpretations of human learning and development. Otherwise, it would be acceptable to base the existence of race on empirical evidence that biology determines culture, without first defining 'race,' and independently determining its existence. Part of the difficulty in refuting false constructions of race is that those biological traits believed to be racial traits are in fact hereditary. However, not everything that is biological or hereditary qualifies as racial—not even according to the most extreme racists. Therefore, the general claim that biological inheritance does not determine human capacities, abilities, or cultural identities, while it may be true on many grounds, is too broad a defense of the nonexistence of race. The breadth of this claim makes it seem as though future empirical findings about the link between biology and culture could confirm the existence of human biological racial taxonomy, which is not the case.

Part of this confusion in the 1998 AAA Statement on "Race," between biology and heredity overall, and race in particular, stems from the lack of a clear definition of what those who believe race is biologically real mean by race. Obviously, the cultural traits distinctive of different so-called races on a geographical basis, as well as the stereotypical traits attributed to subordinate racial populations, are not biologically determined. But the nonscientific belief in biological race is more than a belief in the existence of racially-specific culture and behavior, although that belief about culture and behavior is part of the nonscientific belief about race. The nonscientific belief in biological race entails that there is a biological foundation for distinct racial identity that underlies phenotypes within any race. This assumed biological foundation resembles genealogy, but it is supposed to underlie even genealogy, at least in the United States. Consider the American one-drop rule, which is an exaggerated form of hypodescent: A person is designated racially black if he or she has at least one black ancestor anywhere in family history. Today, the one-drop rule may be justified by reference to either custom or preference, but at the end of the nineteenth century it was justified by a belief that physical racial essences were passed down generationally, through blood. The foundation of the one-drop rule was thus a belief in racial essences, a belief that still lingers despite widespread scientific evidence that no such things have ever existed.[12] The 1998 AAA Statement on "Race" is thus combating the public's false belief in the existence of biological racial essences, but without explicitly addressing this belief.

Biological racial essentialism is different from cultural racial essentialism, whereby stereotypical cultural traits are believed to be the effect of what people believe to be biological race. However, the biological case overrides the cultural case logically (see items 4 and 6 earlier in this section), because what people believe to be biological race in the case of cultural essentialism does not exist. (Beliefs about culture are often themselves lacking in existent referents, but that is another matter.) In science, biological racial essences have gone the way of phlogiston. But the failure of the AAA statement to address the lingering superstition is costly. We are told, "Throughout history whenever different groups have come into contact, they have interbred. The continued sharing of genetic materials has maintained all of humankind as a single species."[13] The implication here is that humankind might not be a single species without continued sharing of genetic material. Indeed, speciation can result from isolated breeding within groups that have common ancestors with other groups. But, if humans never were distinct races to begin with, their maintenance as one species would not be a result of the kind of continued sharing of *racial* genes, as the statement implies. Rather, there has simply been a mixing of *genes* in the history of humankind.

The authors of the 1998 AAA Statement on "Race" are not alone in describing humanity as a whole as inextricably racially mixed. Many who now write about mixed-race identity fall into the confusion of thinking that mixed-race people have varied biological *racial* ancestry. This assumption is evident in an *AN* reference to 2000 U.S. census forms as allowing respondents to identify "more than one" category of race to report diverse ancestry.[14] But, if there are no racial essences, then there are no races in the way the public believes, and there are no things that in combination could result in mixed race in a biological sense (see item 3, above).

Race and Forensic Anthropology

It would in most cases be a distortion to interpret the way in which the idea of race is now used in evolutionary biology, genetics, or biological anthropology as an unspoken or unexamined assumption about the existence of literal racial essences. Those scientists who use concepts that resemble common sense racial categories, such as *mongoloid, negroid,* or *caucasoid,* are usually referring to collections of typical traits shared by members of groups originating in geographical areas at a certain time in the past. As well, most evolutionary models for group membership now rely more on common ancestry than similarity of traits, for classificatory purposes. When scientists do currently speak of races, it is often with qualifications and disclaimers to disassociate their views from nineteenth-century biological essentialism: they are speaking of populations rather than individuals; their conclusions about the traits shared by such groups are no more than statistical or highly probable; the groups identified in genealogical terms, based on genetic analyses, may not resemble common sense racial categories, even though the names for them are similar. Nevertheless, such scientific use of biological concepts of race easily slides into a kind of typology that can be mistaken for the phlogiston kind of racial essentialism. This is because typology itself partly relies on what the eighteenth-century philosopher George Berkeley called *abstract general ideas.* An abstract general idea is supposed to be a symbol for all members of a group, which characterizes each one of them, as a whole entity, in the same way. Berkeley thought that abstract general ideas are tricks of the mind because there is nothing in reality to which they refer. He believed that our idea *man* is an abstract general idea because all men are different, and there is nothing that characterizes every one of them, as wholes, in the same way.[15]

If population and genealogical concepts of race, which apply to groups, are applied to individual members of those groups, then they become abstract general ideas in Berkeley's sense, because there is no one thing or set of things that all members of such groups have in common. Usually, evolutionary biologists and population geneticists do not speak of individuals. However, forensic anthropologists, who classify individuals based on their skeletal remains, have no choice but to speak of individuals, and this is where group-based scientific concepts of race may slide into essentialist concepts of race. The group-based racial term becomes a label for an individual, and by extension it may seem as though every individual in the group to which the new individual has been assigned shares the same defining *something*, in this case a shared group trait. Once this association between group membership and shared group trait becomes established, it may be very difficult to imagine that an individual could be a member of a predescribed geographic or genealogical group if that individual lacks typical traits of the group. However, on either the geographic or genealogical model of human populations, there are bound to be "atypical" members of these groups once the shared similarity model is rejected and, of course, once the notion of group essences has been discarded. The question of whether a given individual is assigned to a group if the individual is atypical will be decided based on whether the criteria for group membership are primarily geographical, osteological, or genetic. This kind of decision highlights the ways in which all typologies are somewhat arbitrary constructions, rather than literal models of natural divisions.

For instance, Leonard Lieberman explains how the nature of the relevant *skeletal reference collection* determines how forensic anthropologists classify new skeletal remains. All of the skeletal traits that compose the typology of skeletal reference collections exist on continua among the different types, and they are usually referred to as *clines* rather than racial traits. This means that the existence of a typology depends on more or less arbitrary decisions about where to draw the lines between types. The criteria for inclusion in types are further contingent in that bones are shaped by environmental, as well as hereditary, factors. Classification therefore works best if unidentified members have ancestors who come from the same geographic area as those in the reference collection.[16] This qualification poses extreme difficulties when remains that are unusual or of unknown origin have to be classified. Given these parameters for forensic anthropology, it is clear that care must be taken not to equivocate between meanings of labels for groups in interpreting data. For example, if a skeletal reference collection is made up of remains of members of groups with no living descendants, there is no basis on which to assume that traits of the group characterize members of living groups who, according to cultural criteria, have been assigned to a race bearing a name similar to the name of the decedent group. Furthermore, as Lieberman points out, the forensic assignment of an individual to any group is only going to be as valid as were the original criteria used in assembling the skeletal reference collection.

The discussion of Kennewick Man in the *Anthropology Newsletter* is an informative example of how the application of population- and genealogical-based ideas of race to human osteological remains sounds like racial essentialism to those who reject common sense racial typology, while it may seem to be no more than normal empirical science to forensic anthropologists who think they can classify given remains. Let's begin with the facts of the case. Kennewick Man is the name given to remains found after flooding of the Columbia River in Kennewick, Washington, in 1996. The skeleton was examined by James Chatters, who identified a well-preserved middle-aged man with apparent 'caucasoid' features who lived about 9,300 years ago. Chatters believes that his preliminary data support hypotheses that there was an earlier, now extinct, European group in the Americas that predated occupation by the North Asian groups believed to be the ancestors of contemporary Native Americans.[17] Chatters and his colleagues anticipated further study of the remains, but the age of the skeleton brought it under the jurisdiction of the Native American Graves Protection and Repatriation Act of 1990. The Army Corp of Engineers removed the skeleton to a secure vault on the assumption that it legally belonged to the Umatilla Indians, tribes in Oregon, Washington, and Idaho, who claimed Kennewick Man for reburial. Chatters and seven colleagues litigated for return of the skeleton to them for further study.[18] (Those are the main facts.)

The Umatilla Indians do not think that further study is desirable because it is against their spiritual traditions to remove the dead from original places of burial. Neither do they think that further study of the skeleton is necessary, because they believe that its age alone establishes its identity as Native American. Thus, Armand Minthorn, speaking for the Umatillas:

> If this individual is truly over 9,000 years old, that only substantiates our belief that he is Native American. From our oral histories, we know that our people have been part of this land since the beginning of time. We do not believe that our people migrated here from another continent, as the scientists do.
>
> We also do not agree with the notion that this individual is Caucasian. Scientists say that because the individual's head measurements does not match ours, he is not Native American. We believe that humans and animals change over time to adapt to their environment. And, our elders have told us that Indian people did not always look the way we look today.[19]

It should be added that practitioners of a Norse religion in California with ideological ties to white supremacist groups have also claimed the skeleton as an ancestor of members of their group, the Asatru Folk Assembly.[20]

The discussion about Kennewick Man in *AN* was published during the same time as other commentary that contributed to the 1998 AAA Statement on "Race." Several issues were intertwined in exchanges about Kennewick Man, and their relation to essentialist versus nonessentialist definitions of race is instructive. First, there was the question of whether the Kennewick remains ought to be made available for study by Euro-American scientists ("was," because the case was decided in favor of the Umatilla Indians in 2001).[21] Then, there is the question of the race of the remains. Finally, there is the issue of what the characteristics of the remains might suggest about precontact populations in the Americas and their geographical origins.

No one in the pages of *AN* offered strong support for reburial of the remains under NAGPRA, and even Alan Goodman, who deplored the racialization of the remains, stated that he would welcome an opportunity to study them without such racialization.[22] Richard Jantz and Douglas Owsley claimed that the Army Corp of Engineers ought not to have seized the remains without "an orderly process" for determining their group identity.[23] It is understandable that empirical scientists would be in favor of further study "no matter what" and that they might tend to dismiss obstacles related to folk claims about identity, as "political." The Umatilla imperative to rebury the remains follows from their presumed Native American identity, and scientists might not wish to give such an imperative priority, insofar as it is merely religious. But, the age of the remains was what triggered their seizure under NAGPRA, and this is related to historical legal principles that cannot be as easily dismissed. U.S. treaty law and legislation such as NAGPRA recognize the precolonial sovereignty of ancestors of contemporary Native Americans. As the only living groups likely to be descended from those erstwhile American sovereign groups, contemporary Native Americans would seem to have a prima facie right to claim remains that could be their ancestors. This would be an argument based on inheritance that bypasses race in any sense of the term. Even if Kennewick Man were (apparently) racially white, he could still have been the ancestor of contemporary Native Americans. The claim by the Asatru Folk Assembly that Kennewick Man could not have been the ancestor of contemporary Native Americans, as well as a possible assumption by some anthropologists that belonging to a Caucasian or caucasoid group precludes Kennewick Man having Native American descendants, would hold up only on the basis of false biological racial essentialism. The essentialist principle would be that Native Americans and whites each have something biologically distinct about them which determines that all descendants will be of the same "race" as their ancestors. Furthermore, even if Kennewick Man were racially white, it is virtually certain that he could not be the ancestor of contemporary racially white Americans, because all of their ancestors arrived after colonial contact. The only way whites, such as the Asatru Assembly, could claim Kennewick Man as their ancestor would be through the nonexistent referent of an abstract general idea of racial whiteness which overrode actual biological genealogy and made every white person a member of the same line of descent; but even in that case, it is likely that members of the Asatru Assembly would be only collateral kin to Kennewick Man.

What race is Kennewick Man? The question is scientifically meaningless if "race" means common sense taxonomies. No one in the *AN* discussion, including the litigating anthropologists, has claimed that if Kennewick Man can conclusively be determined to be caucasoid, it will mean that he is white in common sense racial terms. Everyone acknowledges that the similarity of the population-based terms 'caucasoid,' 'mongoloid,' and 'negroid' to the common sense terms 'white,' 'Asian,' and 'black,' confuses issues of anthropological identification. Thus, Douglas Preston, who wrote a popularized account of the Kennewick Man case for *The New Yorker* magazine, suggested in *AN* that anthropologists could substitute their racial-sounding taxonomy with "Group A," "Group B" and "Group C."[24] Whether or not Preston meant for this suggestion to be taken seriously, it raises an important point. The terms 'caucasoid,' 'mongoloid' and 'negroid,' insofar as they are not essentialist, must refer to presumed places of ancestral origin, both as genealogical beginnings and as evolutionary sources, in terms of environmental adaptation of different skeletal traits that can be used to classify remains. Both ancestral origins and phenotypic differences in groups, which have resulted from environmental adaptation, have been racialized in essentialist constructions of race. This does not mean, however, that the varieties that have been racialized are not in themselves real. That is, the problem is not with words or with the traits to which words refer, but with the *essentializing aspect of racialization*. If the words are changed without addressing false beliefs and meanings that have no empirical referents, after a brief respite, the old false beliefs and meanings will reattach themselves to the new words (or letters).

Nonessentialist population-based typology, although it might have empirical referents, is a weak form of typology, for two reasons. First, as everyone acknowledges, the traits typified are continuous over populations, rather than discretely divided. Second, geographical-origin typology is a matter of decision. There is nothing in nature to indicate how far back one must go to make the right cut to the branches of ancestral groups. Over history, geographically isolated populations continually branch off, in terms of time-spans in different places, which are reflected in genetic difference. As L. Luca Cavalli-Sforza, Paolo Menozzi, and Alberto Piazza describe their own system of human evolutionary branching in *The History and Geography of Human Genes*, "The level at which we stop our classification is completely arbitrary."[25] Thus, if we accept the hypothesis that modern humans originated in Africa, then all human skulls could be classified as 'negroid.' Although, just as we saw in chapter 2 that one race does not constitute a taxonomy of race, one type does not make a typology. Furthermore, on what basis is it decided how many years spent in a place make the traits of inhabitants of that place typical of that particular origin in a defining way? Although a full answer to this question exceeds the scope of this chapter, it is not highly speculative to suggest that evolutionary geneticists make the major cuts in ways that correspond, albeit roughly, to contemporary common sense racial typology. If this speculation is correct, then scientific typology is only as good as the common sense typology on which it is based—which means not very good at all.

Minthorn, speaking for the Umatillas, uses geographical origin to determine human types, a method shared by the anthropologists who typed Kennewick Man as caucasoid: Kennewick Man is Indian for the Umatillas because he comes from the Americas; Kennewick Man is caucasoid for the scientists because he resembles people whose ancestors came from Europe. The main difference in method is that Minthorn does not think the claim that Indians have always inhabited the Americas can be falsified. The oral tradition Minthorn speaks from also posits what scientists might call ad hoc hypotheses of micro-evolution to account for Kennewick Man's caucasoid traits. It is not clear however, whether Minthorn thinks that anyone alive over 9,000 years ago in the Americas is by definition a Native American because of geographical location at that time, or whether Minthorn is, in effect, a polygenicist on the subject of human evolution. His assertion of the folk belief that Native Americans have always been in the Americas would seem to confirm the latter, unless the Umatillas believe that *Homo sapiens* originated in the Americas and migrated to other continents.

Another difference between the Umatillas and the litigating anthropologists is that the Umatillas use what they believe are ultimate geographic origins to type remains, whereas the anthropologists use time slices in ancient history, when relative isolation in different environments resulted in what they can identify as distinct types. There is some question about whether typing in this sense is possible. Those responding to Goodman's assertion that Native American typing cannot be accomplished with accuracy suggest that some methods are more reliable than others.[26] Whatever the method, the size of the sample or skeleton reference collection is crucial. Chatters claims that there is a large enough sample to classify Kennewick Man as a member of a distinct and now extinct group.[27] Duane Anderson, Alan Swedlund, and David Breternitz believe that the sample is small and the Kennewick find does not motivate them to change their classification of a 9,700-year-old female skeleton found in Gordon Creek in 1963 as Native American, despite her possession of what others identify as caucasoid traits.[28]

The population-based identification of Kennewick Man is thus inconclusive, partly because of disagreement about the existence of criteria for classification. And there is the further question of whether or not a caucasoid–Native American typology is even possible. Goodman claims it is not possible because ancient remains often have varied typological traits.[29] Owsley and Jantz insist that the variety within early groups is only apparent and that in cases where it is known that whites and Native Americans were present in the same location, after details of where the remains have been found are taken into account, classification can reliably be carried out.[30] Jonathan Marks, commenting on the disagreement, emphasizes the possibility of what appears to be racial diversity among ancient Native Americans and reports that mitochondrial DNA characteristic of Native Americans has been found in one very old apparently caucasoid skull.[31] What is interesting about the entire discussion among Goodman, Owsley and Jantz, and Marks is that the disagreement stems from two incompatible premises: groups are osteologically distinct; groups are not osteologically distinct. Assuming that the claim about group distinctions is limited to nonessentialist variations that are not racial, it would seem to be an empirical matter whether remains can be classified in any given context, given accepted criteria for classification. But, disagreement about appropriate osteological criteria for classification would need to be resolved on the basis of additional information from archaeology and genetics.

How the ancient Americas were settled, when, and by which group—as minimally defined by where they came from—are empirical questions. The completion of this story would be of broad narrative human interest, but without essentialist ideas of race, it is difficult to see how the story could have nonmetaphorical and (nonrhetorical) political or even identity implications in the present. Kennewick Man and members of his historical-geographical group might have been caucasoid. Caucasoid or not, they might have been ancestors of contemporary Native Americans or unrelated to them. As Chatters himself states, the history of the ancient Americas is turning out to be far more complex than was previously believed.[32] This is hardly surprising, because ancient human history is generally an incomplete inquiry at this time. While writing this section, I read about a BBC program that presented evidence for a hypothesis that the earliest inhabitants of Brazil were a negroid group who originated in Australia. (An archaeological site at Serra De Capivara in northeast Brazil yielded rock paintings believed to be 50,000 years old and a 12,000-year-old skull with apparent negroid features according to forensic reconstruction.[33])

The *AN* discussion about Kennewick Man makes clear the importance of not essentializing geographically based osteological typology. Such typology may be useful to track human migrations historically. But, it is intelligible to the public because it seems to correspond to popular ideas about race. The latter is part of the essentialist problem, generally. Popular ideas of race are based on genetic variation that is (taken to be) dramatic in terms of appearance and in terms of political and economic history, especially colonialism. In terms of biological reality, as Jonathan Friedlaender points out, more reliable population markers can be found in genetic variations of mitochondrial DNA. The groups picked out by those markers provide a different taxonomy than caucasoid-mongoloid-negroid divisions. Still, the mt DNA markers are not present in all members of those populations in which they occur, so typology based on them is also a fabrication beyond "nature."[34] What all of the postessentialist scientific categories of human "racial" groups share *epistemologically* is a certain circularity. Any criterion used to classify members of a group at the same time defines membership in a group. This is because there is no consistent, objective determinant of racial, geographical, osteological, or genetic human group membership, for any group.

Essentialism and Medicine

In the case of Kennewick Man, a distinction between population-based and racialized, skeletal traits would seem to have the effect of making empirical inquiry less fraught, even though it does not mean all human remains can or should be objects of scientific study. In the fields of medicine and public health, the essentialist racialization of people identified as Hispanic, Asian, African American, or white may block useful research into the causes of disease and illness by falsely implying that statistical associations of some debilities with social racial identities has explanatory force on a biological level. If racial distinctions do not exist in human biology then, purely as a matter of logic, biological race cannot be causally linked to physical predispositions for diseases or disabilities. When socially identified racial groups are found to have different diseases or types of illness, which are believed to be directly inherited or the result of inherited "predispositions," this should be the beginning of demographically based medical research and not the end of it. Socially identified race has no medical nomological value when it is linked to disease or illness. If such apparent links come to be generally accepted as signals of the necessity for further research then, eventually, it could be possible to do more than offer treatment for disease (although sometimes the availability of treatment is in itself "racially" unequal). Unequal social conditions that cause different rates of disease could be addressed as a key toward the prevention of certain diseases. Thus, for example, HIV/AIDS has recently been increasing in the African American group while decreasing in other groups. This is a problem that at once requires medical treatment, demographically based research about why blacks are now at greatest risk for AIDS, and social justice remedies should it be the case that specific (and immediately correctable) discrimination against blacks is a factor in these figures.[35]

Among anthropologists and other scientists in human biology, there are now two different approaches to the combination of the facts about human diversity in disease and recognition of the lack of a biological foundation for race. Both approaches require that physiological, genetic, and genealogical data be collected directly from individuals. The first approach accepts a population-based notion of race but questions whether it is possible to determine what populations individuals belong to as a reliable diagnostic tool. For example, when, in 1991 the policy committee of the American Medical Association recommended that all infants be tested for sickle cell anemia, the reasoning was that although sickle cell anemia occurs most frequently among people with Mediterranean and African ancestry, there is no reliable way to independently determine such ancestry.[36] A second example of the association of population typology with disease concerns research on bone marrow compatibility based on human leukocyte antigens (HLAs). Bone marrow compatibility depends on a match in HLAs, and recent studies have confirmed that African Americans and Asian Americans have a large number of HLAs specific to their "racial" groups, while Caucasians, Latin Americans, and Native Americans share a number of common HLAs.[37] The registry of African American donors is disproportionately small. But, African Americans are the most varied in HLAs, so even if the registry for African American donors were very large, some researchers are not confident that transplantation compatibility would increase. They therefore suggest that future resources be concentrated on working with partial compatibilities for hard-to-match recipients.[38] Also, it should be emphasized that when population membership is used to screen potential donors for bone marrow transplants, there has to be individual testing to determine a match for the HLAs in question.

The use of population-based typology for medical research was also assumed in places during the discussion attendant to the AAA Statement on "Race" in *AN*. Thus, Robert Halberstein, writing about research on hypertension, sickle cell anemia, and forensic photography in the Caribbean, argues that phenotypical markers of social race are "unreliable criteria for classifying breeding populations."[39] Halberstein's assumption would seem to be that breeding populations are themselves reliable criteria for the presence of certain diseases. Similarly, Jonathan Friedlaender suggests that the concept of isolated breeding populations that are subject to *random genetic drift* will in the future provide useful explanations for research findings about genetic diversity, particularly in matters of disease.[40]

None of the scientists using populations as units for genetic research on disease suggest that all members of the populations in question have a gene for the disease in question (for example, sickle cell anemia among Africans, Tay-Sachs disease among Ashkenazi Jews) or that no members of other populations may have a particular population-based disease. This means that population membership is neither a sufficient nor a necessary condition for the presence of diseases associated with specific populations. This logical truth means that in terms of individual treatment and diagnosis for population-associated diseases, individuals have to be treated by medical practitioners as though they do not have a particular population membership. Alan Goodman underscores this conclusion by relating how in the 1970s some researchers suggested that because blacks have lower mean hemoglobin concentrations than whites, the standard for the diagnosis of anemia should differ according to race. Goodman notes the danger in this kind of thinking, which was confirmed for the case of hemoglobin by a 1991 discovery that the black-white "racial" difference in hemoglobin concentration was entirely the result of environment.[41]

Goodman's dire caution about the use of population-based categories in medical science is related to his more broad criticism against anything that resembles racial typology in science.[42] In medicine, this is the second approach mentioned at the beginning of this section, an approach to human disease that is not only race-blind concerning a false essentialist notion of race as applied to individuals, but population race-blind also. As already noted, state-of-the-art medical diagnosis would have to be population race-blind in this sense. The broader issue raised by Goodman is whether all human medical research should be population race-blind. An issue broader still, also raised by Goodman, is whether all human evolutionary history, which is constructed on the basis of models of populations who lived in particular places at particular times, can be constructed without typology that resembles false essentialist typologies of race. Goodman thinks it ought to be constructed without such typologies, because of the dangers of retaining false essentialist notions of race, scientifically and socially. I think this brings us back to the end of the previous section. The problem is not with human genetic or geographical variety but with the racialization of that variety in false essentialist ways. The question is whether scientists can be "trusted" to work with population-based typologies in terms of medical research and, more broadly, evolutionary biology without falling into what Goodman calls "the race pit."[43] I do not think that there is a real choice here because there is truth on the side of population statistics and truth on the side of the nonexistence of essentialist racial typologies. After all, it was scientists, who, in addition to having posited false essentialist typologies, collected and interpreted the data about human diversity that proves the impossibilities of such typologies. Scientists are not the only ones who must be trusted not to think in murky ways with false ideas about race. The public needs to be trusted as well, as I will indicate in chapter 7.

7.

Philosophical and Social Implications

Scientific Literacy About Race

The lack of scientific foundation for common sense racial taxonomy presents a challenge to both oppressive and liberatory traditions. Reference to neither the original support by scientists of the oppressive tradition, nor to the history of liberatory humanistic action against this tradition, provides answers to the challenge. Racialist science has proved to be self-correcting, and humanistic liberatory movements should respond to contemporary self-corrected scientific contexts if they are to sincerely continue as liberatory. Such a response is in keeping with the history of resistance among African Americans. Even when black leaders have been religiously motivated and inspired, they have had secular aims that were carried out with intellectual commitment to truth, in opposition to popular superstition.

The public, which is broadly committed to the results of the physical sciences as a source of information about reality, now maintains anachronistic beliefs about race. The present challenge to members of both oppressive and liberatory traditions regarding what they continue to assume about racial taxonomies is, to begin with, an intellectual challenge. In "The Conservation of Races," after Du Bois claimed that the notion of race overflowed the scientific definition of it in 1897, he asserted that the history of the world is the history of races and that "he who ignores or seeks to override the race idea in human history ignores and overrides the central thought of all history."[1] Race lacks the basis in biology assumed by late-nineteenth-century scientists, and as Anthony Appiah showed, by Du Bois himself in his definition of races as families with common histories (see chapter 5). Therefore, it cannot be the case that the history of the world is the history of races. Neither is the history of the world the history of the idea of race, because world history extends further back in time than the modern period, when the idea of biological race was first constructed, and the history of the world that lies ahead will have to take the fact that race is biologically unreal into account—somehow. So, we can now say simply that Du Bois is mistaken here. It is time to put to rest his fantasy that African Americans *could* acquit themselves within a false taxonomy, much less that they *should*.

All of the discussion about science in this book is accessible to educated communities. Most of it is no more difficult to understand than information routinely absorbed in senior high school and introductory college courses. The contemporary information from population genetics, the study of phenotypes, transmission genetics, genealogy, and their relevance to anthropology does not require special talents for absorption by liberal arts educators and their students. What is required is a willingness to acquire scientific literacy relevant to a subject that is one of the major preoccupations of present life in the United States (at least). I would submit that this racially relevant scientific literacy is an obligation for all scholars of race, particularly those who teach and especially those who teach future teachers.

The burning questions evoked by this scientific literacy are social and political. I want to finish the book with suggestions about how those questions can be answered, but, beforehand, some additional philosophical issues need to be addressed: the connection between "race" and "IQ" and race as a social construction.

The Gordian Knot of Race and IQ

As Stephen Jay Gould lucidly notes, assumptions of nonwhite and particularly black intellectual inferiority in comparison to whites have always accompanied modern racial taxonomies. The recurrent debate about the connection between race and IQ is thus no more than a contemporary version of nineteenth-century debates about different racial cranial capacities and intelligence.[2] Ashley Montagu points out that no one can say exactly what intelligence is, and Gould has explained how the notion of a general IQ factor, referred to as *g* or "general intelligence," is highly dependent on the statistical methods used in designing and scoring IQ tests.[3] Nonetheless, the numerical nature of IQ test scores casts an illusory mantle of scientific authority over popularized presentations of statistical correlations between IQ scores and membership in social racial groups. In the 1970s, Arthur Jensen presented arguments against integration and funding programs intended to improve the opportunities of African American schoolchildren, on the grounds that IQ cannot be changed because it is biologically determined in ways that correspond to race.[4] During the 1990s, Robert Herrnstein and Charles Murray presented essentially the same arguments, with more statistics.[5] Montagu notes that both Jensen's and Herrnstein's and Murray's publications appeared at times of federal fiscal retrenchment and should therefore be interpreted as politically motivated.[6] But, though this may be true, it does not address the content of the claims.

IQ, as measured by available tests, is broadly considered to be 60 to 80 percent *heritable* within the white population in the United States. This heritablity of IQ is "the proportion of a population's IQ variability attributable to genes."[7] However, biologists do not equate heritability with biological determinism that is invariant over changing environmental and developmental factors. Height is highly heritable from parents to children within groups if environmental factors are constant, but if dairy products are freely added to diets previously lacking them, the height of a whole generation may increase. Ned Block, among others who have written forcefully about the limits to the genetic component of heritability, painstakingly explicates the ways in which the heritability of a trait does not mean that its expression is independent of environmental conditions.[8] Many evidentiary claims have been made against the conclusions drawn by Jensen and Herrnstein and Murray, including references to studies in which IQ scores have risen as environmental conditions have changed.[9] Furthermore, the 60 to 80 percent heritability figure does not take maternal effects in the womb into account. When those effects are allowed for in statistical studies of identical twins reared apart, the genetic effect on IQ appears to be only 48 percent when the total effect of genes on IQ is calculated. But the genetic effect is only about 34 percent when the additive effect of genes on IQ is calculated and that figure is more relevant in evolutionary arguments.[10]

If conservatives have been strongly motivated to link IQ and race, the liberatory motivation to disprove alleged connections between race and IQ has been passionate. The 1998 American Anthropological Association Statement on "Race" was partly prompted by a desire to correct the public misinformation cast by Herrnstein and Murray's *The Bell Curve*.[11] The 1998 AAA Statement on "Race" began with a claim that biological human races did not exist, as we saw in chapter 6. However, *if races do not exist*, then regardless of whether or not there is some *g* or "general intelligence" factor and regardless of whether, or to what degree, that factor has a genetic component or is heritable, *it is logically impossible that there could be a connection between the genetics of IQ and the genetics of race.* While discussion of the heritability, malleability, and distribution of "intelligence quotients" and of the cultural objectivity of IQ tests is of considerable interest in its own right, such discussion is irrelevant to race in any biological sense.

Race and Social Construction

Publications such as *The Bell Curve* distress many people because they know that there are millions of young African Americans who do not do as well as their white contemporaries on IQ tests. The reasons for that are social, not biological, but in the absence of a biological foundation for racial difference, there seems to be no difficulty in identifying the different groups by race. For this case and other statistically compelling ones, such as race-related differences in public health and imprisonment, it is necessary to give an account of how people are able to sort others into races, and of the coherent persistence of racial identities. Since races are not natural kinds, they must be social constructions, and indeed, mention of the biological emptiness of race is often now followed by the proclamation that race is nothing but a social construction. But that alone is mild news ontologically, because almost all of the important ingredients of contemporary life are social constructions: money, marriage, social class, education, work, gender, beauty, and perhaps even health itself (physical as well as mental). Anything that is the result of human interaction and intention in contexts where past actions, decisions, and agreements have present consequences is, trivially, a social construction. It is therefore necessary to dig a little into the meaning of "social construction" before it can be informative to park race in that category. Ian Hacking observes that the label "social construction" is currently applied to matters of concern to signal that they are not inevitable when it is otherwise assumed that they are inevitable. Imputation of contingency is an important starting point for change, because, usually, the thing asserted to be socially constructed is also believed to be harmful and/or unjust.[12] Hacking also points out that objects, interactions, people in specified social roles or with specific ascribed identities, processes, and results of processes have all been viewed as social constructions in this way.[13] Applying Hacking's insight to race, we could say that each of the following is a social construction: the common sense notion of race, race relations, black, white, Asian, Native American, mixed and any other racial identity, the histories of the foregoing, and the present results of those histories. So far, we know the point of saying that race is a social construction, and we know what particular aspects of "race" are social constructions, but we do not know what constitutes something like race as a social construction, that is, how saying that race is a social construction, can give an account of the way race works in society. We need an answer to this question: If race is not biologically real as people think it is, how does it come to be real in society, which it surely is?

Here is an answer to how race is real in society, but no more than a social construction. Racial taxonomy, or the conceptual scheme whereby everyone belongs to one of three or four races, is a simple scheme of classification, much simpler than astrology, for instance. This taxonomy is taught to children early on in their socialization. Along with the classification go physical, cultural, and psychological stereotypes for each race, which are less complicated than the (astrological) traits of Aquarius, Pisces, Leo, and so forth. More complicated, however, is the epistemology of racial sorting, and that is the most interesting part of the social construction of race. People are sorted into racial categories based on criteria that differ for different races and different individuals within the same race. To consider the big three: blacks require but one black ancestor to be black, but they can have any number of nonblack ancestors; whites require no nonwhite ancestors and a white appearance; Asians require ancestors from a list of countries believed to be "Asian." All of the failed scientific bases of race, except for genetics, which is assumed because it is not visible in ordinary experience, are used to sort people into relevant races. Appearance or phenotype is always the favored criterion, but it has to be confirmed by geographical location of ancestors and the race of an individual's social family. If the sorting cannot be done by direct observation, because the individual is filling out a form, or the individual's appearance is ambiguous, the individual can be asked, directly or indirectly, crudely or with finesse, "What race are you?" Thus, stated racial membership is another criterion (except for cases of "passing").

We can see from this account that first of all, the taxonomy of race, like all taxonomies, is socially constructed in the trivial way. People invented and embellished the taxonomy as a symbolic system. Once the taxonomy was broadly accepted, specific traits of individuals could be used to construct the races of those individuals. Conveniently, racial sorting did not have to take place on an individual basis, but entire geographical groups have been, and still are lined up with components of the taxonomy, for example, inhabitants of Africa were, and still are, designated members of the black race. Racial sorting is a complicated, dynamic system, and since it changes over history and has different nuances within the United States and over the world, it is arbitrary.

However, it is not the problems with the epistemology of race, which qualify it as a social construction in the nontrivial sense, but the fact that the taxonomy of race is itself fictitious—it does not have the physical basis that it is assumed to have. If people viewed race as what used to be called a "parlor game" and did not regard the taxonomy itself as real, there would be no problem with it. It might even be a good social construction in a part of social reality, as many games are. The problematic aspect of race, which underlies what qualifies it as a social construction in the harmful sense that Hacking draws attention to, is twofold: people regard the taxonomy as biologically real; the components of the taxonomy have different connotations of human psychic worth. John Searle's explanation of the construction of social reality, and Jerry Fodor's explanation of token physicalism in the social sciences, provide useful ways in which to compare race with critically nonproblematic, social constructions.

Searle's view is that we live in realities made of physical facts that can be studied in the natural sciences and social facts that are "about" physical facts and other social facts. Language and related symbolic systems connect social facts to physical facts. Social reality has several levels and on each one constructions of facts from levels closer to physical facts occur. These constructions give the facts from more physical levels new meanings on their constructed levels. The new meanings regulate the facts from the previous levels and constitute them as social facts on the new levels. Searle's main example of this process is money. Money as a store of value first occurred in social reality (society) as the precious objects it was, pieces of gold and silver. The instantiation of the general term 'money' by precious objects was a physical fact. The ability of precious objects to instantiate 'money' was a social fact. In time, money came to be nonprecious objects, such as paper, that represented precious objects kept in safe places. Today, money is nonprecious objects and notations that do not represent precious objects and have no value in themselves.[14] Searle's general formula for social construction is X *counts as* Y *in* C, where X is an object, Y is an object, a reason for action, or a symbol, and C is a social context. In counting as Y in C, X comes to have a new status or function that it did not have outside of C. This new status or function, Y, is both constituted and regulated at the same time. Important philosophically is the condition that although X and Y might refer to the same object outside of C, sentences containing X cannot be substituted for sentences containing Y, or vice versa, with preservation of the same truth value. Sentences containing socially constructed terms are *intensional* (in the philosophical sense, with an "s," as Searle puts it).[15]

How does Searle's account work with race? Let skin shade of a certain reflective index, or the existence of an ancestor with skin shade of that reflective index be X. In the context of the United States, X could count as "racially black" (or as "racially white" for a different value of X). This construction has the further stipulation that if an individual has a physical trait, X, that counts for a racial trait, Y, then the entire individual and not just his or her trait is thereby racially constructed. Any criterion for racial membership that has a physical factual basis could be some X that gets constructed as a Y or racial classification. Thus, it is racial membership that is socially constructed in Searle's sense. Of course, the characteristics assigned to different components of the racial taxonomy are also constructed, but that is done all at once on the same symbolic level. If the racial taxonomy corresponded to a biological taxonomy, then race would not be socially constructed; race would be a physical fact.[16] The problem with race as an element of social reality is not so much in the application of the taxonomy but in the nature of the taxonomy itself. The application of the taxonomy is fairly smooth sailing except for borderline cases and cases of mixed race. Race resembles astrology in this way. If you know someone's birth date and the place and hour of her birth, she can be astrologically classified. Because astrology is an ongoing dynamic system based on real, ongoing movements of planets and stars, the original classification can always be preserved by reference to any number of present factors, whenever life or character appears to disconfirm the classification. The problems with astrology lie not in the existence or movements of the planets and stars, and the application of the taxonomy works beautifully. Its problems are that it is based on outdated scientific Ptolemaic assumptions, unjustified causal laws about the influence of planets and stars on human life, and a system of human typing that has no independent justification. Race shares with astrology the absence of justification for its typology, as we have seen in earlier chapters.

The ungrounded aspect of racial taxonomy is also evident if we try to apply Jerry Fodor's notion of *token physicalism* to social race. Fodor is sympathetic to the empiricism of the 'special'—by which he seems to mean 'social'—sciences. Although the predicates in the social sciences would ideally be related to predicates in the physical sciences, ultimately physics, Fodor argues that these predicates cannot be *reduced to* predicates in the physical sciences with preservation of the lawlike structure of the special science that is being reduced. Again, money is a convenient example. There is no way to specify exactly what physical objects or events always correspond to financial transactions, although there is in each individual case some correspondence or 'reduction' of the financial transaction to entities and events that can be described by the predicates of physics. Therefore, Fodor suggests that the special sciences not be required to have a physical base through their predicates or *types*, but through individual instantiations of those predicates or *tokens* of those types. That way, every description of a particular financial transaction, which can be formulated using the predicates of economics, can be equated to a description using the predicates of physics.[17]

In sorting people into races, different kinds of criteria are used for each race and different criteria may be used for individuals within the same race (for example, John is judged to be black because his mother is, whereas Mary is judged to be black because she "looks" black.) Being a member of a race is analogous to being a financial transaction: It can be translated into a biological sentence. But wait! A racialist objection to the claim that race lacks a scientific basis could be made here. If people can be sorted into races in a way that seems to conform to Fodor's model, and his model is good enough for the science of economics in order to ground it as an empirical science, why can't the same thing be said for race? Maybe racial predicates as general terms don't have physical bases, but any given instantiation of any social racial classification has a physical basis, first in biology and perhaps ultimately in physics. Isn't the possibility for such Fodorian token physicalism enough to empirically ground race?

The token physicalist objection would be addressed to all of the foregoing analyses in this book, which led to the conclusion that race lacks a basis in science. But the objection requires a shift in the science in question. Throughout the history of race as a modern system, the science grounding race has been assumed and asserted to be biology, in a direct way. The predicates of race and the divisions in the taxonomy of race were supposed to directly correspond to biological predicates and divisions. Moreover, a whole taxonomy of race was supposed to correspond with some whole taxonomy in biology, so that the racial taxonomy was just another description of the biological taxonomy, and vice versa. Now there could be a "science of race" in which the varied characteristics for membership in this or that race were listed and quantified and qualified, so that a description of each token of a predicate in that racial science could be equated to a description using biological predicates. Such a "science of race" would thereby have to be a special science in its own right, like sociology, psychology, or economics. The cultural dangers of that kind of science exist in the example of the scientific approach to race enacted in Nazi Germany in the 1930s. It is impossible to imagine what social benefits or educational utility could emerge from any special science of race, and I doubt that even the most ardent racialists alive today would be in favor of it. However, the critique of biological race that I have been developing has proceeded independently of moral argument, so the pernicious quality of a "science of race" is not enough to rule it out in this context. It is the criteria for what counts as a science that would rule out a "science of race" in Fodor's terms: A "science of race" would not qualify as a special science because it could not have well-formed empirical predicates. We have already established the lack of biological referents for racial taxonomies and specific races. So the predicates of the science of race could not be biological. If they were social, it is impossible to imagine what the generalizations and laws of those predicates could be, as a first order science.[18] Of course, there can be and are areas within the special or social sciences that are understood to be about beliefs and intentions about social race. That is, race can be and is studied in sociology, psychology, anthropology, history, and even economics.

To sum up, as symbolic systems, taxonomies of race are social constructions in a trivial sense, but the applications of those taxonomies to human variety require complex practices of social construction that are philosophically interesting and nontrivial. The purported connections and disconnections between assumed biological taxonomies and human talents and culture are a further social construction and deconstruction. Thus, not only is race as a social construction not inevitable, but it has gone through at least one major change in proof of its "evitability." The concept of a paradigm affords a useful theoretical perspective on the changing nature of social constructions of race.

The ingredients of a racial paradigm at any given time would include a taxonomy of race, the criteria for membership in different races and their application to individuals, social customs and laws that pertain to race, moral beliefs about different race relations, expectations for change in social areas pertaining to race, ideologies of race, and beliefs about the connections between physical race and human psychic attributes. Because beliefs, rules, practices, and formal social structures are all parts of it, a racial paradigm is not merely a symbolic system but its accompanying life world, as well. From this theoretical perspective, we can distinguish at least three paradigms of race. The first, from the late eighteenth century to the early twentieth, had hierarchical racial taxonomies favoring whites, which rankings were believed to be unchanging and morally just. Different human psychic capacities and their expressions were held to be determined by racial heredity, as were physical characteristics.

The second paradigm of race took up most of the twentieth century, and except for revisions in the biological sciences, where they were previously racialist, and philosophical inquiries such as this one, it remains culturally dominant. Ideas of human psychic endowments have been disengaged from physical racial taxonomies. The white-supremacist customs and institutional practices that were considered morally right under the first paradigm have been subjected to intense criticism, with considerable progress toward their elimination.

The third paradigm of race would be the last one. Its core positive belief and principle underlying action is that race is biologically unreal. Once social racial taxonomies are eliminated, the correction of racialist white-supremacist customs and institutional practices would continue. But, the theoretical basis on which they are corrected will likely move away from direct or emic conceptualizations of race, in favor of the descriptions of beliefs and empirical descriptions of economic and social inequalities that can be addressed by changes in education and public policy.[19]

Finally, before leaving the subject of race as social construction, something should be said about nominalism. Is the position that race is unreal a nominalist position? Although this question arises naturally enough, it is misdirected. Nominalism is a general doctrine about what gives terms their meanings or what the source of meanings is. It makes sense only if applied to terms that are properly presupposed to refer to existent objects. In emic contemporary usage, that could be said about the term 'race,' but not in the etic sense following the knowledge that race lacks the foundation in biology that it is supposed to have emically. One can be a nominalist about chairs, ice cream, breeds of dogs, and even species of animals, but not about the Tooth Fairy, Santa Claus, or astrology. Nominalism is too weak a way of saying that something is unreal. Similarly, like John Locke, one can be a nominalist about the method of classification used for borderline cases, provided that the mainline classifications are well formed. If there were races, one could be a nominalist about exactly how many races there were or about how to classify mixed-race people. But one cannot be a nominalist about race insofar as it purports to have a biological foundation that it lacks.[20]

Social Justice Implications

Race is not biologically real as most people still think, but the existence of racism past and present cannot be denied. There is no paradox here. People believe that race is real, and their belief has been enlivened by greed, fear, anger, and cruelty that often have nothing to do with race, as a motivating idea. But the belief in race has also itself been sufficient to occasion distinctive emotions, motives, and moral attitudes. The results have been racist psychic states and dispositions and racist practices. Racism has been the main use for the social construction of race.

Racism consists of individual and social preferences and aversions based on different racial identities. It has both deliberate forms and socially mechanistic ones that perpetuate themselves in the apparent absence of ill will toward victims. For example, some philosophy professors assume that African American students are not likely to want to learn philosophy, so they reserve their intensive pedagogy for white students. Over their careers, these academics tend not to recruit many or any African American philosophy majors or graduate students. Over time, the field of philosophy does not change in its predominantly white membership. Where blacks were once explicitly excluded as a consequence of their more general exclusion from higher education, they now simply—not that anything like this is ever simple—continue to fail to develop enduring interests in philosophy.[21] Furthermore, some philosophers do not believe that the present situation is racist, because many of the white philosophers involved do not have self-acknowledged feelings of hatred, aversion, or contempt for blacks. But if one views the situation in terms of a concept of institutional racism, it is racist.

When victims of racism racially identify themselves in order to resist and combat racism, they positively affirm the very identities that are used by racists in ways that have victimized them. Even if they have *transvalued* the oppressive identities within communities of resistance, the identities still refer back to their racialist or racist origins. There would be no point to the transvaluation if external racism did not exist as something to be resisted and overcome. If racial identities were biological facts, then those identities would not be part of racial injustice. Racial identities have not been biological facts as those are understood by biologists since the early twentieth century, and persistent racial taxonomies depend on an ontological commitment to the existence of race as something that can be studied by science. Moreover, all racial taxonomies make a division between whites and nonwhites, which was originally posited by European whites for their own advantage. For these reasons, the affirmation of nonwhite identities probably has an intrinsic ceiling concerning the degree of justice that it can achieve. Such affirmation has been the road most traveled ever since Du Bois cautioned American blacks against minimizing racial difference, because he believed that they needed to strive to fulfill the destiny of their race.[22]

The lack of a biological basis for race is not a political issue. Still, interested parties will want to know exactly how that information will affect the politics of race as it has thus far developed in the service of social justice. If politics is a struggle for power and advantage or decreased disadvantage, the scientific facts are irrelevant unless they can be translated into motivating and empowering rhetoric. For such rhetorical purposes, emic racial identities are probably more useful because they require less intellectual effort to evoke. But stating it this way expresses a cynical condescension toward politicians, activists, and their public(s). Politics, political action, and rhetoric should be principled, with the aim of bettering the human condition and not merely obtaining more desirable relations of power. The core of good politics is a commitment to the life and dignity of all human beings. Such universalism would be compatible with common sense racial taxonomy if it were a system of mere variety and not one of value-laden difference. Twentieth-century liberatory racial politics was a series of footnotes to Du Bois played out as an insistence on the compatibility of existing racial taxonomy (containing an ontological commitment to biological race) with universal equality. Many liberatory and radical activists and scholars of race do not trust whites not to discriminate and behave unjustly to nonwhites unless nonwhite racial identities are explicitly mentioned, noticed, and acknowledged. Legal critical race theorists have argued that the race-neutral language of egalitarian law does not address existing racism, because it assumes it is possible to view all citizens as though they had no racial identities. In fact, unquestioned and pervasive discrimination on the basis of race often excludes nonwhites completely, so that contexts in apparent compliance with legal race neutrality are often contexts inhabited exclusively by whites.[23] The resulting political strategy has been to insist on visible and recognized nonwhite racial identities as integral ingredients in a new democratic pluralism.

What would happen if it became common knowledge that race in the emic biological sense did not exist? Possibly, new pseudobiological grounds for discrimination and aversion would be constructed. Certainly, there would continue to be social injustice against the poor, because they are the most vulnerable component of the capitalistic global corporate enterprise. But it is an empirical question exactly whether and how the present victims of racism might benefit from being relieved of false biological identities. It will require great courage to allow such a question to be answered through the actions of others, whom those most concerned with outcomes have no direct influence over and small reason to trust. The individual and small group project of relinquishing false biological notions of race will have two phases. The first is the acquisition and distribution of the required information about human biology. This scientific literacy will proceed at a slow pace through the academy until it is disseminated at the secondary and primary school levels. On the way, the resistance of the mass media to educated opinion that is not sensationalistic about race will have to be worn down, something that will probably happen only as the three-race generation is replaced by the no-race generation in research, business, and policy-making positions. That is the cognitive phase of the project.

The second phase of relinquishing false biological notions of race is the practical one of rethinking, undoing, and redoing those aspects of ordinary life and discourse, both oppressive and liberatory, which rely on assumptions that racial taxonomies and individual racial differences are real in ways that can be studied by biology. This revision will require a reexamination of received texts and the discovery and creation of new ones in many different fields. So far, the racial liberatory focus has been confined to issues of racism and reactions against it. Needed now will be concentration on the ways in which ungrounded taxonomies of race inform discourse. It will be necessary to reach a lucid understanding of what it literally and metaphorically means to use words and phrases such as these: black, Indian, Jewish, or any kind of racial blood, bloodlines, mixed blood, pure blood, racial solidarity, brotherhood, sisterhood, black ancestry, racial heritage, racial identity, or racial authenticity. These are just a few polite examples.

Discourse affects perception. It has become a sign of astuteness for African Americans to claim that when they look into the mirror, they do not see a man or woman before the glass, but a black man or a black woman. It has also become a sign of social awareness for everyone to notice whether or not a group or institution is racially diverse. Both self-perception and the perception of others as racially identified presuppose that racial identity is given in perception, whether one makes a point of noticing it or not. Suppose one looked at oneself and others and merely noted those physical characteristics that are used to socially construct race, without thereby constructing race? What will we see? How will what we see affect the humanity we take for granted or withhold from ourselves and others?

Where general discourse is embedded with a persistent idea, the idea has an effect on actions and institutions that go beyond the medium of discourse. For instance, is it racism that keeps the United States residentially segregated, or might it not also at core be *racialism*? Much more would be at stake in the shift from the second to the last paradigm of race, than cognition, perception, discourse, and social habit. Economics and politics would be involved, and it is money that could speed up a process of cultural change otherwise requiring centuries. It is not a coincidence that the widespread presence of women in the American workplace accompanied the shift from a manufacturing to an informational and service economy during a period of inflation that made it necessary for women to contribute to household income. Slavery was a profitable form of agricultural business for the South, and during the period of intense segregation, blacks in the workforce continued to be exploited by whites who despised them socially and excluded them politically. The hatred and genocide of Native Americans accompanied their dispossession from ancestral lands. In the West, during the late nineteenth and early twentieth centuries, Asian immigrants were a source of cheap labor for railroad construction and agriculture, and they were treated with great cruelty and contempt. Today, disproportionate numbers of African Americans are "in" the criminal justice system, and some critics now call it "the prison industrial complex," because inmates represent jobs for prison personnel and profits for contractors.

I don't want to milk what alert adolescents now know or put too great a burden on neo-Marxian insights. But, it is important to realize that while the racial identities assigned to those exploited have oiled the wheels of exploitation, those identities have often been extrinsic and ad hoc to the brute facts of exploitation. It couldn't have been otherwise, given that there never existed any such thing as biological race. The more brutal the exploitation, the greater the vilification of its victims by those benefiting from their servitude and death. The fulcrum for historical change on behalf of the victims of exploitation is not a matter of how they are identified before, during, or after exploitation, but the material conditions that make them vulnerable to exploitation in the first place. Because American economic exploitation is mostly a matter of profit, and the business of America is still business, material conditions are most of the story. This subject exceeds the scope of this book, but it is the next subject after the disabuse of "race."[24]

As a practice, the revision of biological ideas of race will reach so deeply into lives based on racial affinities and aversions that the world will not merely become a more just place in issues of race, but it will no longer be the same world.[25] Even the most dedicated and idealistically motivated, and especially them, barely have enough minutes in the day to fulfill their present work, family, social, and civic obligations. How will they have time to effect such change, and with little thanks at the outset? As the practical project of revising life worlds imbued with false ideas of race progresses, it will free up the time and effort presently consumed by race. Because race is a construction requiring constant sorting and identification, it is a dynamic, ongoing, performative process. There is nothing about anyone's racial membership that is simply attached once. Racial membership must constantly be tended, remembered, enacted, and reenacted. Some nonracial part of consciousness must always be ready to assess what is required from a racial self. Under Jim Crow, black men had to remember not to look at white women, and today they have to remember not to scare white women if they encounter them alone at night on city streets. Whites have to remember that they can count on certain unearned advantages that increase directly with the degree of racism in the context. Asian Americans have to remember to let white Americans know that they were born in the United States and to forgive them for assuming that they were instead born somewhere "in Asia." As I revise this manuscript, the current war following September 11, 2001, is contributing to many things that Islamic Americans will have to remember about how they are perceived. Children of all races need to be periodically reminded of their racial membership and of what their elders consider to be the obligations or "dues" that accompany it. Given all this, it's probably not a matter of finding the time to undo race, but of appreciating in retrospect how much time was spent doing it, and making good use of the resources thus liberated.

In immediate pragmatic terms, interested parties will want to know how, while this great revision is occurring, they are expected to view contemporary laws against racial discrimination, as well as the remnants of affirmative action. Will the acknowledged demise of biological race render such measures redundant? I think that anyone who is familiar with race relations in the United States, both past and present, anyone who lives in the culture with a modicum of awareness of how advantages and disadvantages get distributed, would sense that the acknowledged biological emptiness of race is no guarantee that old epistemologies of common sense race won't continue to operate, or that biological race will not still be constructed. But the construction will be driven underground. Once again witchcraft provides a thought experiment. Witches were believed to be real, the majority thought that they could identify them, and when it was convenient, they tormented and persecuted them. After it came to be generally acknowledged that witches did not exist, it was witch hunters and witch tormentors, in a word, "witchists," who were on the defensive. Even private social discrimination against witches in cultures failing to believe that witches existed would be difficult to imagine. We have already seen such a process at work between the first and second paradigms of race. The first paradigm belief that inferior psyches and cultures accompanied nonwhite racial identities has been rejected as an unacceptable form of racism under the second paradigm. However, the pragmatic answer to the above question is that all of the laws protecting nonwhites against racism, and probably more such laws, are necessary until racism no longer exists, *no matter how long that takes*. In short, racism must be treated separately from the facts about race, even though the facts about race represent its ultimate demise, now in theory, later in practice.

The Stakes

During the mid 1990s, an erudite and well-published African philosopher of my acquaintance, who had been an American citizen for several years, applied to be nominated for a university affirmative action position in a department of philosophy, also of my acquaintance. The candidate gave a talk about his work to the philosophy department and was interviewed on campus. The members of the philosophy department who participated in the interviewing process were all white males. Much to his disappointment, the candidate was not accepted for nomination by the philosophy department, because they did not think he was "really" a philosopher. He was a mature man, much traveled, and educated in England, so he was aware first-hand of the history of colonialism and postcolonialism in Africa and beyond. He said to me, "Oh, I know these white guys from way back. They don't change much. Maybe an inch a century."

There remains much ongoing institutional racism in the United States, as well as recalcitrant pockets of overt and deliberate individual racism against nonwhites. However, given that the public still lives within a racial paradigm, the civil rights, voting rights, and immigration rights secured by nonwhites in the United States over the twentieth century are at least an inch of change. The next inch will have to be gained first within educated liberatory movements that have disabused themselves of empirically ungrounded biological notions of race, races, racial identities, and individual racial projects.

To end with the direct question about stakes posed in the Introduction. Some will say, "So what if race is a social construction? Ordinary racist life will not be disturbed by this so-called news of the lack of biological foundation." How do they know that this news will have no effect, when the belief that race is biological is embedded in "race" as a social construction? Race is like the liar who says he speaks the truth, the social construction that is constructed around denial that it is a social construction.

The notion of race as biological is not an abstract fact that is independent of other vital beliefs held by people. Race as biological has been a vast network of practical ideas and thought, which to name a few includes: ideals of beauty, sexuality and forms of gender, notions of special skills, ideas about character, virtue, vice, wealth, the family, and superiority and inferiority. And each of those ideas and more has been lived out in emotion, experience, and behavior.

Du Bois's envisioned dawn was an idea of legal equality and economic and educational opportunity for blacks in America. The civil rights legislation of the 1960s was the historical face of Du Bois's dawn. That time has been succeeded by morning and the fatigue of late morning. We are now at a High Noon, when war, terror, new projects of racialization, the complete corporate colonization of the world, and its attendant ecological depletion, demand a degree of vigilance, against which attachment to identities based on outdated science is frivolous. It would also be frivolous for me, here, to attempt further *rhetoric* toward getting those who think 'left' to recognize a basic scientific truth about humankind. Those to the 'right' are still not off the hook concerning institutional racism. We should all think straight about this matter that runs deeper than politics.

Notes

Introduction

1. See Editor's Introduction; Keith S. Donnellan, "Reference and Definite Descriptions"; and Saul Kripke, "Identity and Necessity," in *Naming, Necessity and Natural Kinds*, ed. Stephen P. Schwartz (Ithaca, NY: Cornell University Press, 1977).
2. William K. Goosens, "Underlying Trait Terms," in Schwartz, *Naming, Necessity and Natural Kinds*.
3. See K. Anthony Appiah, "Race, Culture, Identity: Misunderstood Connections," in *Color Conscious: The Political Morality of Race*, ed. Stephen P. Schwartz and Amy Gutmann (Princeton, NJ: Princeton University Press, 1996), pp. 40–42.
4. See Naomi Zack, "Race and Philosophic Meaning," in *RACE/SEX: Their Sameness, Difference and Interplay*, ed. Naomi Zack (New York: Routledge, 1997).
5. Richard H. Popkin, *The History of Skepticism from Erasmus to Spinoza* (Berkeley: University of California Press, 1979); Naomi Zack, *Bachelors of Science: Seventeenth Century Identity, Then and Now* (Philadelphia: Temple University Press, 1996), chapter 3.
6. On the question of realism of sexual dimorphism, see Judith Butler, *Gender Trouble: Feminism and the Subversion of Identity* (New York: Routledge, 1990), pp. 106–11.
5. However, in philosophy of science, the topic is usually called realism rather than social construction. See for instance Jerold L. Aronson, Rom Harre, and Eileen Cornell Way, *Realism Rescued* (Chicago: Open Court, 1995); Janet A. Kourany, ed., *Scientific Knowledge: Basic Issues in the Philosophy of Science* (Belmont, CA: Wadsworth, 1998), part 4, "Realism vs. Anti-Realism: The Ontological Import of Scientific Knowledge."
7. Richard Lewontin, *The Triple Helix* (Cambridge, MA: Harvard University Press, 2000), pp. 69–107.

Chapter 1: Philosophical Racial Essentialism: Hume and Kant

1. Berel Lang, "Metaphysical Racism (Or: Biological Warfare by Other Means)," in *RACE/SEX: Their Sameness, Difference and Interplay*, ed. Naomi Zack (New York: Routledge, 1997).
2. Naomi Zack, "Philosophy and Racial Paradigms," *The Journal of Value Inquiry* 33 (1999): 299–317.
3. John Relethford suggested the following, based on a hypothesis of C. Loring Brace, in review comments on this chapter: Explorers, who preceded colonists, traveled long distances to arrive at locations of populations new to Europeans. Human groups are dissimilar in direct proportion to the distance between them, so groups far apart would likely support taxonomies based on extremes. However, this suggestion leaves unanswered the ques-

tion of why a taxonomy based on extremes that was biased in favor of Europeans would be congenial to Europeans at that point in their history.

4. Aristotle, *Metaphysics* 1031, b 18–22. Aristotle's discussion of essences occurs mainly in book 4, chapters 4, 5, 6. Aristotle, *Basic Works*, ed. W. D. Ross, trans. Richard Mckeon (New York: Random House, 1941), pp. 787–91.

5. Elliott Sober, "Evolution, Population Thinking and Essentialism," in *Conceptual Issues in Evolutionary Biology*, ed. Elliott Sober (Cambridge, MA: MIT Press, 1997).

6. John Locke, *An Essay Concerning Human Understanding*, ed. Peter H. Niddich (Oxford: Oxford University Press, 1975), book 2, chapter 6. S. 13–20, pp. 447–49.

7. Ibid., book 2, chapter 6, S. 36, p. 462.

8. Irving M. Copi, "Essence and Accident," in *Naming, Necessity and Natural Kinds* ed. Stephen P. Schwartz (Ithaca, NY: Cornell University Press, 1977).

9. Copi, "Essence and Accident"; also Sober, "Evolution, Population Thinking and Essentialism."

10. Ivan Hannaford, *Race: The History of an Idea in the West* (Baltimore, MD: Johns Hopkins University Press, 1996), pp. 48–49.

11. John Locke, *A Letter Concerning Toleration*, ed. James H. Tully (Indianapolis, IN: Hackett, 1983), 52. For further discussion of the ways in which Locke lacked a concept of biological race, see Naomi Zack, *Bachelors of Science: Seventeenth Century Identity, Then and Now* (Philadelphia: Temple University Press, 1996), chapter 12, "Slavery without Race." John Locke *Essay*, book 2, chapter 6, S. 13–20, pp. 447–49.

12. Locke, *Essay*, book 2, chapter 6, S. 22–23, pp. 450–52.

13. See Zack, *Bachelors of Science*, chapter 12, "Slavery without Race."

14. Locke, *Essay*, book 2, xxvii, 8, p. 333.

15. Nigel Tattersfield, *The Forgotten Trade* (London: Jonathan Cape, 1991), p. 11.

16. A seminal article on this point, also reiterated in statements issued by UNESCO in the 1950s, was Claude Lévi-Strauss, "Race and History," in *Race, Science and Society*, ed. Leo Kuper (New York: Columbia University Press, 1965). For the UNESCO statements see the Appendix in Kuper. More recently, members of the American Anthropological Association thought it necessary to underscore the point in their 1998 "AAA Statement on 'Race.'" *Anthropology Newsletter* 39, no. 9 (September 1998): 3. See chapter 6 in this volume for an analysis of that statement.

17. David Hume, "Of National Characters," in *Essays Moral, Political and Literary*, ed. T. H. Green and T. H. Grose (London: Longmans, Green and Col, 1875), 2 vols. Essay XXI (see pp. 85, 252 for dates of editions).

18. Richard H. Popkin, "Hume's Racism," *Philosophical Forum* 9/2 nos. 2–3 (Winter-Spring, 1977–78): 211–26. For Buffon's views see George-Louis Leclerc, Comte de Buffon, "The Geographical and Cultural Distribution of Mankind," from *A Natural History, General and Particular*, reprinted in *Race and the Enlightenment: A Reader*, ed. Emmanuel Chukwudi Eze (Cambridge, MA: Blackwell Publishers, 1997), pp. 15–28.

19. Hume, "Of National Characters," pp. 244–49 (quote from p. 249).

20. Ibid. pp. 249–52.

21. Ibid. p. 252.

22. Popkin, "Hume's Racism," cited n. 17, pp. 215–16.

23. David Hume, "Of the Populousness of Ancient Nations," in Green and Grose, *Essays*, p. 382. (See p. 56 of the *Essays* for the history of this essay.) Essay XI, pp. 381–42.

24. Hume, "Populousness," p. 249.

25. James Beattie, "A Response to Hume," from *An Essay on the Nature and Immutability of Truth, in Opposition to Sophistry and Skepticism*, reprinted in Eze, *Race and the Enlightenment*, pp. 34–37.

26. Beattie, "A Response to Hume," p. 37.

27. Immanuel Kant, "On the Different Races of Man," in *This Is Race: An Anthology Selected from the International Literature on the Races of Man*, ed. Earl W. Count (New York: Henry Schuman, 1950), p. 16.

28. See chapters 2 and 3, in this book, for more complete discussion of the contemporary biological science consensus about human genealogical diversity and its evolutionary origins, and chapter 4 for a discussion of racial phenotypes.

29. See Michael Ruse, *Philosophy of Biology Today* (Albany: State University of New York Press, 1988), p. 59.

30. Kant, "On the Different Races of Man," in Count, *This Is Race*, p. 17.

31. Ibid.

32. See Ranier Spencer, *Spurious Issues: Race and Multiracial Identity Politics in the United States* (Boulder, CO: Westview, 1999); Naomi Zack, "Mixed Black and White Race and Public Policy," in *Race, Class, Gender and Sexuality: The Big Questions*, ed. Naomi Zack et al. (Malden, MA: Blackwell Publishers, 1998).

33. See Alain Corcos, *The Myth of Human Races* (East Lansing: Michigan State University Press, 1997), pp. 3, 175–77; Richard Lewontin, *The Triple Helix* (Cambridge, MA: Harvard University Press, 2000), p. 120.

34. Ibid., p. 19

35. Ibid. p. 17.

36. Philip Kitcher, "Race, Ethnicity, Biology, Culture," in *Racism*, ed. Leonard Harris (New York: Routledge, 1998).

37. For discussion of Kant's distinction between the "twin sciences" of geography and anthropology, see Emmanuel Chukwudi Eze, "The Color of Reason: The Idea of 'Race' in Kant's Anthropology," in *Anthropology and the German Enlightenment*, ed. Katherine Faull (London: Bucknell and Associates University Press, 1994).

38. Immanuel Kant, *Anthropology from a Pragmatic Point of View*, ed. Hans H. Rudnick, trans. Victor Lyle Dowdell (Carbondale: Southern Illinois University Press, 1996), p. 3.

39. Eze, "The Color of Reason," in Faull, *Anthropology and the German Enlightenment*, 216, trans. by Eze from Friedrich Christian Stare, *Kant's Philosophische Anthropologie: Nachhandschriftlichen Vorlesungen* (Leipzig, 1831), p. 353.

40. Kant, "On National Characters," in Eze, *Race and the Enlightenment*, pp. 55–56.

41. Quoted by Richard K. Popkin in "Hume's Racism," in *The Philosophical Forum* 9, nos 2–3 (winter-spring, 1997–98): 218, from Immanuel Kant, *Observations on the Feeling of the Beautiful and the Sublime*, trans. John T. Goldthwait (Berkeley: University of California Press, 1965), pp. 110–11.

42. On the teleological role of history for Enlightenment rationalism, see David

R. Hiley, *Philosophy in Question: Essays on a Pyrrhonian Theme* (Chicago: University of Chicago Press, 1988), pp. 58–60.

43. See Kwame Anthony Appiah, "Racisms," in *Anatomy of Racism*, ed. David Theo Goldberg (Minneapolis: University of Minnesota Press, 1990). I skipped a step in applying Appiah's distinction between intrinsic and extrinsic racism. Appiah defines intrinsic racism as the belief that mere membership in a race confers moral qualities, extrinsic racism as the belief that racial membership conveys moral qualities through the medium of a racial essence. However, since Appiah's notion of extrinsic racism entails that a rational extrinsic racist could change his or her beliefs, given evidence that members of a race do not have the moral qualities ascribed to them, it would follow that the ascription of moral qualities to a race could be falsified. This aside, the aspect of Hume and Kant's thought which I am emphasizing here is their belief that there are human races, an ontological position presupposed by both the extrinsic and intrinsic kinds of racism.

Chapter 2: Geography and Ideas of Race

1. Thanks to John Relethford for making the explicit connections expressed in the last two sentences of this paragraph in his review comments.

2. Ashley Montagu, *The Idea of Race* (Lincoln: University of Nebraska Press, 1965), chapter 3, pp. 81–116; *The Concept of Race*, ed. Ashley Montagu (New York: Free Press of Glencoe, Macmillan, 1964), Introduction, pp. xii–xviii.

3. For a useful collection of eighteenth- and nineteenth-century theories of white supremacy, including writing, by Thomas Jefferson, Comte de Buffon, Hume, Kant, and Hegel, see Emmanuel Chukwudi Eze, ed. *Race and the Enlightenment: A Reader* (Cambridge, MA: Blackwell Publishers, 1997).

4. See Stephen Jay Gould, *The Mismeasure of Man* (New York: Norton, 1996).

5. Claude Lévi-Strauss, "Race and History," in *Race, Science and Society*, ed. Leo Kuper (New York: Columbia University Press, 1965), pp. 95–134.

6. Amerigo Vespucci, *Mundus Novis*, reprinted in *Philosophy in the 16th and 17th Centuries*, ed. Richard H. Popkin (New York: Free Press, 1966), p. 26.

7. George-Louis Leclerc, Comte de Buffon, *A Natural History, General and Particular*, reprinted in Eze, *Race and the Enlightenment*, pp. 20–21.

8. Johann Friedrich Blumenbach, "Degeneration of the Species," from *On the Natural Varieties of Mankind*, reprinted in Eze, *Race and the Enlightenment*, pp. 82–83.

9. Georg Wilhelm Fredrich Hegel, "Geographical Bases of World History," from *Lectures on the Philosophy of World History*, reprinted in Eze, *Race and the Enlightenment*, pp. 148–49.

10. Ibid., p. 124.

11. Daniel G. Blackburn, "Why Race Is Not a Biological Concept," in *Race and Racism in Theory and Practice*, ed. Berel Lang (Lanham MD: Rowman and Littlefield, 2000), pp. 3–26, especially pp. 13–14.

12. Richard R. Popkin, "Hume's Racism," in *Philosophy and the Civilizing Arts: Essays Presented to Herbert W. Schneider*, ed. Craig Walton and John P. Anton (Athens: Ohio University Press, 1974), pp. 150–51.

13. See Milford Wolpoff and Rachel Caspari, *Race and Human Evolution* (New York: Simon and Schuster, 1997), chapter 6, pp. 136–72.

14. Ibid. See also Milford H. Wolpoff, John Hawks, and Rachel Caspari, "Multiregional, Not Multiple Origins," *American Journal of Physical Anthropology* 112 (2000): 129–36. See also Blackburn, "Why Race Is Not a Biological Concept"; John Noble Wilfred, "Skulls in Caucasus Linked to Early Humans in Africa," *New York Times*, May 12, 2000, p. A1.

15. Luigi Luca Cavalli-Sforza, *Genes, Peoples and Languages*, trans. Mark Seielstad (New York: Northpoint Press, 2000), pp. 57–66.

16. Blackburn, "Why Race Is Not a Biological Concept," p. 18.

17. See John H. Relethford, "Models, Predictions and the Fossil Record of Modern Human Origins," *Evolutionary Anthropology* 8 (1999):7–10; Wolpoff and Caspari, *Race and Human Evolution*, especially pp. 257–59.

18. Cavalli-Sforza, *Genes, Peoples and Languages*, pp. 61–66; See also Richard Preston, "The Genome Warrior: Craig Venter's Race to Break the Genetic Code," *The New Yorker*, June 12, 2000, pp. 66–77.

19. John H. Relethford, *Genetics and the Search for Modern Human Origins* (New York: Wiley-Liss, 2001), pp. 194–211; Lynn B. Jorde, Michael Bamshad, and Alan R. Rogers, "Using Mitochondrial and Nuclear DNA Markers to Reconstruct Human Evolution," *BioEssays* 20 (1998): 126–36.

20. Relethford, however, who is a multiregionalist, thinks that skull proportions, although not skin reflectance, may be a reliable index of population history, because craniometric variation among modern human populations, while showing a low variation among groups, varies about the same amount among groups as do genetic markers. (See Relethford, "Craniometric Variation Among Modern Human Populations," *American Journal of Physical Anthropology* 95 [1994]: 53–62.) However, it is difficult to understand how a statistical correlation between genetic marker differences and craniometric indices could mean that craniometrics is a reliable index of population history without either an independent phenotypic basis for population taxonomy that privileged craniometrics, or an explanation of some causal link between genetic markers, which do not influence somatic development and craniometrics. Furthermore, as noted, on the multiregional hypothesis, there is little reason to think that any population has a single ancestry, on account of gene flow.

21. Cavalli-Sforza, *Genes, Peoples and Languages*, pp. 61–66.

22. Ibid.

23. Ibid.

24. Jorde et al., "Using Mitochondrial and Nuclear DNA Markers to Reconstruct Human Evolution," *BioEssays*.

25. Cavalli-Sforza, *Genes, Peoples and Languages*, pp. 77–82.

26. Nicholas Wade, "The Human Family Tree: 10 Adams and 18 Eves," *New York Times*, May 2, 2000, p. F1.

27. Cavalli-Sforza, *Genes, Peoples and Languages*, pp. 82–85.

28. For different versions of multiregional and replacement or out-of-Africa theories, see Relethford, *Genetics and the Search for Modern Human Origins*, pp. 67–81; Jorde et al., "Using Mitochondrial and Nuclear DNA Markers"; Alan R. Rogers and Lynn B. Jorde, "Genetic Evidence on Modern Human Origins," *Human Biology* 67 (1995):1–36.

29. See note 20, above.

30. An interesting anachronistic theme in this regard is expressed in Charles

Mills's rhetorical attempt to interpret modern European hegemony as a "racial contract" by projecting later biological notions of race onto early colonialist and mercantilist ideologies and political philosophies. Mills attempts to use European and American social contract theory (from Locke to Rawls) to explain Western white supremacy. However, the victims and objects of colonialism did not consent to their enslavement and exploitation in the informed way that social contract theory would require, and there is no trace of irony or even sarcasm in Mills's polemics on this score. (Charles W. Mills, *The Racial Contract* [Ithaca, NY: Cornell University Press, 1997.])

31. Lewis Gordon, *Existentia Africana* (New York: Routledge, 2000), pp. 82–83.

32. Gordon goes even further than this with his claim that African Americans have "long been able to see" that the physical traits of some whites indicate their African ancestral origins and thereby vouchsafe their "Negro" identities. Gordon believes that all human genetic diversity existed in the original African population and that through selective breeding, that population developed into apparently different races. He thinks that nonetheless the group designated "Negro" today has greater genetic diversity than any other group. One wonders how Gordon can say both that everyone is black and that the group designated as black is different from other groups in diversity, but that contradiction could be overlooked had Gordon not overlooked, or failed to notice, the presently well-publicized fact that any small human population, anywhere on earth, now contains most of the diversity in the human genome (see chapter 4, below, for a discussion of the last; see *Existentia Africana*, p. 83, for what I have here attributed to Gordon). There is also a moral dimension to Gordon's version of population genetics. He says that blackness is synonymous with humanity. Gordon seems not to have advanced scholarly discussion of race and science beyond the place secured when Eldridge Cleaver retold Elijah Muhammad's myth about Dr. Jacob, a black scientist who bred "the white devil with the blue eyes of death" from an original (angelic?) black population. (See Eldridge Cleaver, *Soul on Ice* [New York: Dell, 1968], p. 99.) Such rhetoric, no matter how self-intoxicating or otherwise therapeutic it may be, does no more than switch the poles of insult from white to black and black to white, without, sadly, testing the ground supposed to support them.

33. Cavalli-Sforza, *Genes, Peoples and Languages*, chapter 5. See also Luigi Luca Cavalli-Sforza and Francesco Cavalli-Sforza, *The Great Human Diaspora* (Menlo Park, CA: Addison-Wesley, 1995).

34. Robin O. Andreasen, "A New Perspective on the Race Debate," *British Journal of Philosophy of Science* 49 (1998): 199–225.

35. Cavalli-Sforza, *Genes, Peoples and Languages*, pp. 57–85.

36. See Alain Corcos, *The Myth of Human Races* (East Lansing: Michigan State University Press, 1997), pp. 83–88.

Chapter 3: Phenotypes and Ideas of Race

1. Luigi Luca Cavalli-Sforza, *Genes, Peoples and Languages*, trans. Mark Seielstad (New York: Northpoint Press, 2000), pp. 83–85.

2. Nina G. Jablonski and George Chaplin, "The Evolution of Human Skin Coloration," *Journal of Human Evolution* 39, no. 1 (July 2000): 57–106.

3. John H. Relethford, *The Human Species: An Introduction to Biological Anthropology* (Mountain View, CA: Mayfield, 1997), p. 403.

4. N. P. Dubunin, "Race and Contemporary Genetics," in *Race, Science and Society*, ed. Leo Kuper (New York: Columbia University Press, 1975), pp. 68–94.

5. Charles Darwin, *The Descent of Man and Selection in Relation to Sex* (1871); chapter 7, "On the Races of Man," reprinted in *The Idea of Race*, ed. Robert Bernasconi and Tommy L. Lott (Indianapolis, IN: Hackett, 2000); Ashley Montagu, *The Idea of Race* (Lincoln: University of Nebraska Press, 1965), pp. 97–98.

6. Darwin, *Descent of Man*, p. 72.

7. See Stephen Jay Gould, *The Mismeasure of Man* (New York: Norton, 1981); John H. Haller Jr., *Outcasts from Evolution: Scientific Attitudes of Racial Inferiority, 1859–1900* (Carbondale: Southern Illinois University Press, 1995); Audrey Smedley, *Race in North America: Origin and Evolution of a Worldview* (Boulder, CO: Westview Press, 1999), chapters 10, 11, and 12.

8. Ashley Montagu, ed., *The Concept of Race* (New York: Free Press of Glencoe, Macmillan, 1964), pp. 261–62.

9. Alain Corcos, *The Myth of Human Races* (East Lansing: Michigan State University Press, 1997), pp. 194–98. It has been known for some time that determination of the number of genes involved in apparent skin color is not simple, because earlier studies have assumed that mating is random in mixed populations and there is a factor of arbitrariness in deciding how many phenotypic classifications have to be accounted for. See P. J. Byard and F. C. Lees, "Estimating the Number of Loci Determining Skin Colour in a Hybrid Population," *Annals of Human Biology* no. 1 (1981): 49–58.

10. See J. Blangero, L. Almasy, R. Duggirala, S. Williams-Blangero, P. O. Connell, and M. P. Stern, "Mapping Quantitative Trait Loci Influencing Normal Human Variation: The Genetics of Skin Reflectance," *American Journal of Physical Anthropology*, Supplement 28 (1999): 93–94.

11. Richard Lewontin, *The Triple Helix: Gene, Organism and Environment* (Cambridge, MA: Harvard University Press, 2000), chapters 1 and 2.

12. Relethford, *The Human Species*, pp. 402–3.

13. Ashley H. Robins, *Biological Perspectives on Human Pigmentation* (Cambridge, UK: Cambridge University Press, 1991), pp. 5–11.

14. Ibid., pp. 11–12.

15. Ibid., p. 18.

16. Ibid., pp. 12–19.

17. Ibid., p. 12.

18. Arthur Ernest Mourant, *The Distribution of the Human Blood Groups* (Oxford UK: Blackwell, 1954), pp. 1–5; Alexander S. Weiner, "Anthropological Investigations on the Blood Groups," in *This Is Race: An Anthology Selected from the International Literature on the Races of Man*, ed. Earl W. Count (New York: Henry Schuman, 1950), pp. 679–87.

19. Weiner, "Anthropological Investigations," p. 687.

20. Ibid., p. 679.

21. *The Wadsworth Dictionary of Science and Technology* (Ware, Hertfordshire, UK: Wadsworth Editions Ltd., 1995), p. 2.

22. L. C. Dunn, "Race and Biology," in Kuper, *Race, Science and Society*, p. 56.

23. Adapted from Dunn and from Relethford, *The Human Species*, p. 43.
24. Richard Lewontin, *Human Diversity* (New York: Scientific American Library, 1995), p. 42.
25. Mourant, *The Distribution of the Human Blood Groups*, pp. 6–29.
26. Lewontin, *Human Diversity*, p. 46.
27. Cavalli-Sforza, *Genes, People and Language*, pp. 15–17. Also, Mourant, n. 25, above.
28. Smedley, *Race in North America*, pp. 305–6; Relethford, *The Human Species*, pp. 64–66.
29. A. M. Brues, *People and Race* (New York: Macmillan), p. 1.
30. See note 27, above.
31. Dubunin, "Race and Contemporary Genetics," pp. 74–76.
32. Daniel C. Blackburn, "Why Race Is Not a Biological Concept," in *Race and Racism in Theory and Practice*, ed. Berel Lang (Lanham, MD: Rowman and Littlefield, 2000), pp. 1–27.
33. Luigi Luca Cavalli-Sforza, Paolo Menozzi, and Alberto Piazza, *The History and Geography of Human Genes* (Princeton, NJ: Princeton University Press, 1994), abridged paperback edition, p. 9.
34. Luigi Luca Cavalli-Sforza and Francesco Cavalli-Sforza, *The Great Human Diasporas: The History of Diversity and Evolution* (Reading, MA: Addison Wesley, 1995), pp. 112–18; Cavalli-Sforza et al., *The History and Geography of Human Genes*, pp. 68–83.
35. Cavalli-Sforza et al., *The History and Geography of Human Genes*, p. 19.
36. Relethford, *The Human Species*, pp. 387–97.
37. Cavalli-Sforza, *Genes, Peoples and Languages*, pp. 46–48.
38. J. Clinton Jarrett, "From the Agency for Health Care Policy and Research," *Journal of the American Medical Association* 70, no. 18 (1991): 2158.
39. Relethford, *The Human Species*, p. 392.
40. Ibid., pp. 93–94.
41. C. Loring Brace, "Nonracial Approach Towards Human Diversity," in Montagu, *The Concept of Race*, p. 107.
42. Ibid., pp. 119–46.
43. Cavalli-Sforza and Cavalli-Sforza, *The Great Human Diasporas*, pp. 10–14.
44. Gould, *The Mismeasure of Man*.
45. See note 7, above.
46. Montagu, *The Idea of Race*, p. 71.

Chapter 4: Transmission Genetics and Ideas of Race

1. See at the least, Ernst Mayr, *The Growth of Biological Thought: Diversity, Evolution and Inheritance* (Cambridge, MA: Belknap Press of Harvard University Press, 1982).
2. See International Human Genome Sequencing Consortium, "Initial Sequencing and Analysis of the Human Genome," *Nature* 409 (February 15, 2001): 860–92, especially p. 860.
3. On the 6 percent figure for the percentage of human species variation within social races, see Alan R. Templeton, "Human Races: A Genetic and Evolutionary Perspective," *American Anthropologist* 100, no. 3 (1998): 632–51;

On the 10 percent figure, see Guido Barbujani, Arianna Magagni, Eric Minch, and L. Luca Cavalli-Sforza, "An Apportionment of Human DNA Diversity," *Proceedings of the National Academy of Science, USA.* 94 (1997): 4516–519.

4. My account is a simplified version of the one in John H. Relethford, *The Human Species: An Introduction to Biological Anthropology* (Mountain View, CA: Mayfield, 1990), pp. 29–51. It hasn't differed much from the account I learned as an undergraduate in the 1960s, and it is also readily available in encyclopedia articles and many high school biology textbooks.

5. For the complexity and contingency of the influence of genetics on pheno-types, see Richard Lewontin, *The Triple Helix: Gene, Organism and Environment* (Cambridge, MA: Harvard University Press, 2001), especially pp. 1–68.

6. See Relethford, *The Human Species*, pp. 29–51.

7. Ibid., p. 46.

8. Mayr, *Growth of Biological Thought*, p. 292

9. Relethford, *The Human Species*, pp. 29–51; Crossing over tends to take place at the ends or "arms" of chromosomes; see International Consortium, "Initial Sequencing," p. 861–62.

10. Alan H. Goodman, "Six Wrongs of Racial Science," in *Race in 21st Century America*, ed., Curtis Stokes, Theresa Melendez, and Genice Rhodes-Reed (East Lansing: Michigan State University Press, 2001), pp. 26–27; Mayr, *Growth of Biological Thought*, pp. 84–94.

11. Mayr, *Growth of Biological Thought*, pp. 256–60.

12. Ibid. p. 260.

13. Ibid. That Mayr did not discuss race in an extensive nineteenth-century history of biological thought written in 1981 may be an omission of interest to social critics of science, but in this context it provides invaluable independent evidence of how scientific studies of heredity during the nineteenth century were embedded with concepts that when applied to race supported what we would today consider to be racist perspectives.

14. See note 10, above.

15. See chapter 1, above; Naomi Zack, "Race and Philosophic Meaning," in *Race and Racism*, ed. Bernard Boxill (Oxford, UK: Oxford University Press, 2001), pp. 43–58.

16. Mayr, *Growth of Biological Thought*, pp. 48–50.

17. See note 10, above.

18. Mayr, *Growth of Biological Thought*, pp. 635, 693–94, 697.

19. Ibid., pp. 695–794.

20. L. C. Dunn and Theo Dobzhansky, *Heredity, Race and Society: A Scientific Explanation of Human Difference* (New York: Mentor Books, 1952), p. 15; Daniel J. Kevles, *In the Name of Eugenics: Genetics and the Uses of Human Heredity* (Berkeley: University of California Press, 1985), pp. 3–20.

21. Mayr, *Growth of Biological Thought*, p. 784.

22. Ibid., pp. 670–71, 723–24.

23. See K. Anthony Appiah, "Race, Culture, Identity: Misunderstood Connections," in *Color Conscious: The Political Morality of Race*, ed. K. Anthony Appiah and Amy Gutmann (Princeton, NJ: Princeton University Press, 1996), pp. 3–106.

24. Mayr, *Growth of Biological Thought*, pp. 695–98.

25. Ibid., p. 552.

26. Ibid., p. 636.

27. Goodman, "Six Wrongs," p. 37.

28. Joel Williamson, *New People* (New York: Free Press, 1980); Willard B. Gatewood, *Aristocrats of Color* (Bloomington: Indiana University Press, 1990).

29. See Natalie Angier, *New York Times*, February 13, 2001, pp. F1, F5.

30. See International Human Genome Sequencing Consortium, "Initial Sequencing and Analysis of the Human Genome," *Nature* 409, 860–921 (February 15, 2001): especially 860–64.

31. Emma Ross, "Europe Finds Its Roots in Africa," Associated Press, printed in *Times Union*. Albany, NY, April 21, 2001, pp. A1 and A8.

32. Natalie Angier, "Do Races Differ? Not Really, Genes Show," *New York Times*, August 22, 2000, p. F1.

33. Ibid., p. F1.

34. On the distinction between genetic and census population sizes, see John H. Relethford, *Genetics and the Search for Modern Human Origins* (New York: Wiley-Liss, 2001).

35. Audrey Smedley, *Race in North America: Origin and Evolution of a Worldview* (Boulder, CO: Westview Press, 1999), pp. 303–18.

36. Alice M. Brues, *People and Races* (New York: Macmillan, 1977), p. 1 (cited in Smedley, *Race in North America*, p. 312, in John H. Relethford, *The Human Species: An Introduction to Anthropology* (Mountain View, CA: Mayfield), 1990, p. 359.

37. Cited in Goodman, "Six Wrongs," p. 29 (from George W. Gill, "A Forensic Anthropologist's View of the Race Concept," abstract, *American Academy of Forensic Sciences*, 46th Annual Meetings, 1994, p. 163).

38. Goodman, "Six Wrongs," pp. 29–30.

39. Luigi Luca Cavalli-Sforza and Francesco Cavalli-Sforza, *The Great Human Diaspora*, trans. Sara Thorne (Reading, MA: Addison Wesley, 1995), pp. 97–101.

40. John H. Relethford, *The Human Species: An Introduction to Biological Anthropology* (Mountain View, CA: Mayfield, 1990), pp. 72, 82, 387–94.

41. Patrick G. Beatty, Motomo Mori, and Edgar Milford, "Impact of Racial Genetic Polymorphism on the Probability of Finding an HLA-Matched Donor," *Transplantation* 60, no. 8 (October 27, 1995): 778–83.

42. For these problems with populations, see Alain Corcos, *The Myth of Human Races* (East Lansing: Michigan State University Press, 1995), pp. 103–9; Relethford, *Human Species*, pp. 63–68, 479–87; Smedley, *Race in North America*, pp. 303–10.

43. See Naomi Zack, "American Mixed Race: The 2001 Census and Related Issues," *Harvard Blackletter Law Journal* 17 (Spring, 2001), pp. 33–46.

44. *Loving v. Virginia*, *United States Reports*, vol. 388, Cases Adjudged in the Supreme Court at October Term, 1966. Washington DC: United States Government Printing Office, 1968, p. 11.

45. Frantz Fanon, *Black Skin, White Masks* (New York: Grove, 1967), p. 111.

46. Steve Olson, "The Genetic Archaeology of Race," *Atlantic Monthly* (April, 2001). Web posting, www.theatlantic.com/issues/2001/04/olson, pp. 1–7, quote from p. 2.

Chapter 5: Genealogy and Ideas of Race

1. See chapter 3 for a more extensive discussion of clines. As already noted Ashley Montagu defined a cline as: "A gradient in a measurable genetic character within groups of animals or plants, and correlated with a gradient in the climate, geography or ecology of the groups." Ashley Montagu, ed., *The Concept of Race* (New York: Free Press of Glencoe, 1964), pp. 261–62.

2. Willi Hennig, *Grundzüge einer Theorie der Phylogenetischen Systematik* (Berlin: Deutscher Zentralverlag, 1950), cited in Ernst Mayr, *The Growth of Biological Thought: Diversity, Evolution and Inheritance* (Cambridge, MA: Belknap Press of Harvard University Press, 1982), p. 226.

3. Mayr, *Growth of Biological Thought*, p. 227.

4. Ibid., pp. 227–30.

5. Robin O. Andreasen, "A New Perspective on the Race Debate," *British Journal of the Philosophy of Science* 49 (1998): 199–225. See also the discussion of Cavalli-Sforza's research in chapter 2, above.

6. Nina G. Jablonski and George Chaplin, "The Evolution of Human Skin Coloration," *Journal of Human Evolution* 39, no. 1 (July 2000): 57–106 (quote from abstract, p. 58).

7. Mayr, *Growth of Biological Thought*, pp. 226–30.

8. On moral obligation based on racial membership, see Barbara Hall, "The Libertarian Role Model and the Burden of Uplifting the Race," in *Women of Color and Philosophy*, ed. Naomi Zack (Malden, MA: Blackwell, 2000), pp. 168–81. On racial intermarriage from African American perspectives, see Anita L. Allen, "Interracial Marriage: Folk Ethics in Contemporary Philosophy," in Zack, *Women of Color*, pp. 182–296, and Charles W. Mills, "Do Black Men Have a Moral Duty to Marry Black Women," in *Reflections: An Anthology of African American Philosophy*, ed. James A. Montmarquet and William H. Hardy (Belmont, CA: Wadsworth, 2000), pp. 167–82. On reasons not to be morally obligated by racial membership, see Jason D. Hill, *Becoming a Cosmopolitan: What It Means to Be a Human Being in the New Millennium* (Lanham, MD: Rowman and Littlefield, 2000).

9. W. E. B. Du Bois, "The Conservation of Races," reprinted in Robert Bernasconi and Tommy L. Lott, *The Idea of Race* (Indianapolis, IN: Hackett, 2000), pp. 108–17.

10. Ibid., p. 109.

11. Ibid., p. 110.

12. Ibid.

13. K. Anthony Appiah, "The Uncompleted Argument: Du Bois and the Illusion of Race," in Bernasconi and Lott, *The Idea of Race*, pp. 188–235. See also Appiah, *In My Father's House* (Oxford, UK: Oxford University Press, 1992) and "Race, Culture, Identity," in Appiah and Gutmann, *Color Conscious: The Political Morality of Race* (Princeton, NJ: Princeton University Press, 1996), pp. 1–73.

14. Appiah, "The Uncompleted Argument," pp. 124–25.

15. Du Bois, "The Conservation of Races." "Blood" as an important aspect of race is mentioned several times on at least these pages: 110, 111, 112, and 115.

16. See chapter 1, above.

17. Appiah, "The Uncompleted Argument," p. 133.

18. Du Bois, "The Conservation of Races," p. 114.

19. Peter Loptson, *Theories of Human Nature* (Peterborough, Ontario, Canada: Broadview Press, 1995), pp. 10–11.

20. Appiah, "The Uncompleted Argument," p. 135.

21. On taxonomies with large numbers of races, see S. M. Garn, *Human Races* (Springfield, IL: Charles C. Thomas, 1965). See also John H. Relethford, *The Human Species: An Introduction to Biological Anthropology* (Mountain View, CA: Mayfield, 1997), chapter 14, "Human Micro-Evolution."

22. On racial identity and family identity, see Naomi Zack, *Race and Mixed Race* (Philadelpha: Temple University Press, 1993), chapters 3, 4, and 5.

23. Anita Allen, "Interracial Marriage," pp. 182–296.

24. For discussion of American miscegenation under slavery, see James Kinney, *Amalgamation!* (Westport, CT: Greenwood, 1985); Robert J. Sickels, *Race, Marriage and the Law* (Albuquerque: University of New Mexico Press, 1972); Joel Williamson, *New People* (New York: Free Press, 1980); Zack, *Race and Mixed Race*, chapter 8, pp. 77–85.

25. Eugene A. Foster, M. A. Jobling, P. G. Taylor, P. Donnelly, P. de Knijffs, Rene Mieremet, T. Zerjal, and C. Tyler-Smith, "Jefferson Fathered Slave's Last Child," *Nature* 396 (November 5, 1998): 27–28. For accounts of the story before it was corroborated by the DNA comparisons, see Fawn M. Brodie, *Thomas Jefferson: An Intimate History* (New York: Norton, 1974); Shanon Lanier, *Jefferson's Children: The Story of One American Family* (New York: Random House, 2000).

26. For a discussion of other members of Jefferson's paternal line as possible fathers of Eston, see David M. Abbey et al., "The Thomas Jefferson Paternity Case," in Correspondence *Nature* 397 (January 7, 1999): 32.

27. Foster et al., ibid. See also Madison J. Gray, "A Founding Father and His Family Ties: DNA Test Extends Jefferson Legacy," *New York Times*, March 3, 2001, pp. B1, B6.

28. See Lanier, *Jefferson's Children*.

29. See Gray, "A Founding Father and His Family Ties."

30. See for instance John Seabrook, "DNA Testing and the Mania for Genealogy," *The New Yorker*, March 26, 2001, pp. 58–71.

31. See Carey Goldberg, "DNA Offers Link to Black History: Promise in Tracing African-American Ancestry Before Slavery," *New York Times*, August 28, 2000, p. A10.

32. *Loving v. Virginia*, 388 *U.S. Reports* 1 (1968).

33. For accounts and analyses of the varied experiences and forms of mixed race in the United States, see Maria P. P. Root, ed., *Racially Mixed People in America* (Newbury Park, CA: Sage, 1992), and Root, ed., *The Multiracial Experience: Racial Borders as the New Frontier* (Newbury Park, CA: Sage, 1996); Naomi Zack, ed., *American Mixed Race: The Culture of Microdiversity* (Lanham, MD: Rowman and Littlefield, 1995).

34. Bureau of the Census, U.S. Department of Commerce, United States Census 2000, form D1(UL) (2000). For an outline of the census history, see David Theo Goldberg, "Made in the USA," in Zack, *American Mixed Race*, pp. 237–57.

35. See Maria P. P. Root, "The Multiracial Experience: Racial Borders as a Sig-

nificant Frontier in Race Relations," in Root, *The Multicultural Experience*, pp. xiii–xxviii.

36. Eric Schmitt, "For 7 Million People in Census, One Race Category Isn't Enough," *New York Times*, March 13, 2001, p. A1.

Chapter 6: Race and Contemporary Anthropology

1. "Is It 'Race'? Anthropology on Human Diversity," in *Anthropology Newsletter* 38, no. 4 (1997): 5.

2. Audrey Smedley, "Origins of Race" *Anthropology Newsletter* 38, no. 11 (1997): 52.

3. Yolanda Moses, "An Idea Whose Time Has Come Again," *Anthropology Newsletter* 38, no. 10 (1997): 4.

4. American Anthropological Association, "1998 AAA Statement on 'Race,'" *Anthropology Newsletter* 39, no. 9 (1998): 3.

5. K. Anthony Appiah, "Race, Culture, Identity: Misunderstood Connections," in *Color Conscious: The Political Morality of Race*, ed. K. Anthony Appiah and Amy Gutmann (Princeton, NJ: Princeton University Press, 1996), pp. 68–69. Alan R. Templeton, "Human Races: A Genetic and Evolutionary Perspective," *American Anthropologist*, 100, no. 3 (1998): 632–31.

6. Jonathan Marks, external reviewer comments sent in 2000 to *Anthropological Theory*, in which a different version of the material in this chapter was published as Naomi Zack, "Philosophical Aspects of the AAA Statement on Race." See acknowledgments to this book, for a full citation.

7. American Anthropological Association, "1998 AAA Statement on 'Race,'" *Anthropology Newsletter* 39, no. 9 (1998): 3.

8. Claude Lévi-Strauss, "Race and History" in *Race, Science and Society*, ed. Leo Kuper (New York: Columbia University Press, 1965), pp. 95–134.

9. UNESCO, "Four Statements on the Race Question" in Kuper, *Race, Science and Society*, pp. 341–65.

10. UNESCO, "3 Proposals on the Biological Aspects of Race," written in Moscow, 1964, in Kuper, *Race, Science and Society*, p. 358.

11. My point 6 is also made by Yolanda Moses; see note 3, above.

12. See James Kinney, *Amalgamation!* (Westport, CT: Greenwood Press, 1985); John C. Mencke, *Mulattoes and Race Mixture* (Ann Arbor: University of Michigan Institute of Research Press, 1979); Naomi Zack, *Race and Mixed Race* (Philadelphia: Temple University Press, 1993), chapter 8, and Naomi Zack, *Thinking About Race* (Belmont, CA: Wadsworth, 1998), chapter 1.

13. American Anthropological Association, "1998 AAA Statement on 'Race,'" *Anthropology Newsletter* 39, no. 9 (1998): 31.

14. Mary Margaret Overby, "AAA Tells Feds to Eliminate 'Race,'" *Anthropology Newsletter* 38, no. 10 (1997): 1.

15. George Berkeley, *A Treatise Concerning the Principles of Human Understanding*, ed. Kenneth P. Winkler (Indianapolis, IN: Hackett, 1982), pp. 9–14, par. 9–14.

16. Leonard Lieberman, "Out of Our Skulls? Caucasoid? Mongoloid? Negroid?" *Anthropology Newsletter* 38, no. 12 (1997): 56.

17. Douglas Preston, "The Lost Man," *The New Yorker*, June 16, 1997, pp. 70–81.

18. James Chatters, "Human Biological History, *Not* Race," *Anthropology Newsletter* 39, no. 2 (1998): 19.

19. Minthorn's text is partly quoted by Preston in "The Lost Man" in *The New Yorker* and the full text available at the Umatilla tribe URL consulted August 1999: http://www.umatilla.nsn.us/kennman.html.

20. *Runestone* URL consulted August 1999: http://www.runestone.org/km.html.

21. Avila A. Brandt, "Burial, Not Research for Ancient Remains," *Associated Press*, September 26, 2000.

22. Alan Goodman, "Racializing Kennewick Man," *Anthropology Newsletter* 38, no. 10 (1997): 3.

23. Richard Jantz and Douglas Owsley, "Polemicizing Kennewick Man" *Anthropology Newsletter* 9, no. 3 (1998): 56.

24. Douglas Preston, "Kennewick's Message of Unification," *Anthropological Newsletter* 38, no. 12 (1997): 2.

25. L. Luca Cavalli-Sforza, Paolo Menozzi, and Alberto Piazza, *The History and Geography of Human Genes* (Princeton, NJ: Princeton University Press, 1996), p. 19.

26. Alan Goodman, "Racializing Kennewick Man," p. 3.

27. James Chatters, "Human Biological History, *Not* Race," p. 19.

28. Duane Anderson, Alan Swedlund, and David Breterniz, "Let's Avoid Paleo-racial Anthropology," *Anthropology Newsletter* 38, no. 12 (1997): 13.

29. Alan Goodman, "Racializing Kennewick Man," p. 3.

30. Richard Jantz and Douglas Owsley, "Polemicizing Kennewick Man," p. 56.

31. Jonathan Marks, "Replaying the Race Card," *Anthropology Newsletter* 39, no. 5 (1998): 1.

32. James Chatters, "Human Biological History, *Not* Race," p. 19.

33. BBC Two (1999) "First Americans Were Australians," program, "Ancient Voices: The Hunt for the First Americans." September 2, 1999.

34. Jonathan Friedlaender, "Commentary: A Perspective on Race in Biology and Medicine," *Anthropology Newsletter* 38, no. 12 (1997): 48.

35. Ira Harrison, "HIV/AIDS Crisis in the African-American Community," *Anthropology Newsletter* 39, no. 5 (1998): 7.

36. Clinton J. Jarret, "From the Agency for Health Care Policy and Research," *Journal of the American Medical Association* 70, no. 18 (1991): 2158.

37. National Marrow Donor Program Registry, and Motomi Mori, Patrick G. Beatty, Michael Graves, Kenneth M. Boucher, and Edgar L. Milford, "HLA Gene and Haplotype Frequencies in the North American Population," *Transplantation* 64, no. 7 (1997): 1017–27.

38. Patrick G. Beatty, Motomo Mori, and Edgar L. Milford "Impact of Racial Genetic Polymorphism on the Probability of Finding an HLA-Matched Donor," *Transplantation* 60, no. 8 (1995): 778–83.

39. Robert Halberstein, "Commentary: The Race Concept and Research on Human Variation in Medical Anthropology," *Anthropology Newsletter* 38, no. 11 (1997): 45.

40. Jonathan Friedlaender, "Commentary," p. 48.

41. Alan Goodman, "The Race Pit," *Anthropology Newsletter* 39, no. 5 (1998): 41.

42. Ibid.

43. Ibid.

Chapter 7: Philosophical and Social Implications

1. W. E. B. Du Bois, "The Conservation of Races," in *The Idea of Race*, ed. Robert Bernasconi and Tommy L. Lott (Indianapolis, IN: Hackett, 2000), p. 110.

2. Stephen J. Gould, "Racist Arguments and IQ" in *Race and IQ: Expanded Edition*, ed. Ashley Montagu (New York: Oxford University Press, 1999), pp. 183–89.

3. Ashley Montagu, "Introduction" in *Race and IQ*, p. 1; Stephen Jay Gould, "Critique of the Bell Curve," in Gould, *The Mismeasure of Man* (New York: W.W. Norton, 1996), pp. 367–90.

4. A. R. Jensen, *Educability and Group Differences* (New York: Harper and Row, 1973).

5. R. J. Herrnstein and Charles Murray, *The Bell Curve* (New York: The Free Press, 1994).

6. Gould, "Racist Arguments and IQ," p. 189, n. 1.

7. B. Devlin, Michael Daniels, and Kathryn Roeder, "The Heritability of IQ," *Nature* 388, no. 31 (July 1997): 468–71.

8. Ned Block, "How Heredity Misleads About Race," in Montagu, *Race and IQ*, pp. 444–81.

9. Ibid.

10. Ibid.

11. American Anthropological Association, "Should the AAA Adopt a Position Paper on 'Race?'" *Anthropology Newsletter* 38, no. 7 (1997): 27.

12. See Ian Hacking, *The Social Construction of What?* (Cambridge, MA: Harvard University Press, 1999), pp. 5–8ff.

13. Ibid., pp. 8–62.

14. John Searle, *The Construction of Social Reality* (New York: The Free Press, 1995), pp. 48–58, 79–112.

15. Ibid., pp. 18–19.

16. Earlier, I presented a different application of Searle's theory of social construction to race, but I think the one here is better. See Naomi Zack, "Philosophy and Racial Paradigms," *The Journal of Value Inquiry* 33 (1999): 299–317 (my earlier application is on pp. 308–9).

17. Jerry Fodor, "Special Sciences, or The Disunity of Science as a Working Hypothesis," *Synthese* 28 (1974): 77–113.

18. Thanks to Bradford Z. Mahon for reminding me of this.

19. For a more comprehensive discussion of race and paradigm theory, see Zack, "Philosophy and Racial Paradigms." loc. cit. note 16.

20. For a more comprehensive treatment of the meaning of race, see Naomi Zack, "Race and Philosophic Meaning," *American Philosophical Association Newsletter on Philosophy and the Black Experience* 94, no. 1 (Fall 1994): 11–18, reprinted in *Race and Racism*, ed. Bernard Boxill (Oxford, UK: Oxford University Press, 2001), pp. 43–57.

21. See Leonard Harris, "The Status of Blacks in Academic Philosophy," *The Journal of Blacks in Higher Education* (Winter, 1994/5), reprinted in *Race, Class, Gender and Sexuality: The Big Questions*, ed. Naomi Zack, Laurie Schrage, and Crispin Sartwell (Malden, MA: Blackwell, 1998), pp. 48–49.

22. W. E. B. Du Bois, "The Conservation of Races," reprinted in *The Idea of*

Race, ed. Robert Bernasconi and Tommy L. Lott (Indianapolis, IN: Hackett, 2000), pp. 108–17.

23. On these issues, see Patricia J. Williams, *The Alchemy of Race and Rights* (Cambridge, MA: Harvard University Press, 1991).

24. On these issues, see Naomi Zack, "Lockean Money, Globalism and Indigenism," *Canadian Journal of Philosophy, 1999 Supplementary vol. 25*; Catherine Wilson, ed., *Civilization and Oppression* (Calgary: University of Calgary Press, 1999), pp. 31–53; Zack, "Goldberg on Segregation and Prisons," *African Philosophy* 13, no. 2 (2000): 164–71.

25. See Hacking, *The Social Construction of What?*, pp. 128–32.

Select Bibliography

American Anthropological Association. "1998 AAA Statement on 'Race.'" *Anthropology Newsletter* 39, no. 9 (September 1998): 3.

Andreasen, Robin O. "A New Perspective on the Race Debate." *British Journal of Philosophy of Science* 49 (1998): 199–225.

Angier, Natalie, "Do Races Really Matter?" *New York Times*, August 22, 2000, pp. F1, F5.

Appiah, K. Anthony, and Amy Gutmann. *Color Conscious: The Political Morality of Race.* Princeton, NJ: Princeton University Press, 1996.

Aristotle, *Metaphysics* 1031, b 18–22. Aristotle, *Basic Works*. Edited by Richard Mckeon. Translated by W. D. Ross. New York: Random House, 1941.

Bernasconi, Robert, and Tommy Lott, eds. *The Idea of Race.* Indianapolis, IN: Hackett, 2000.

Blackburn, Daniel G. "Why Race Is Not a Biological Concept." In *Race and Racism in Theory and Practice*, edited by Berel Lang. Lanham, MD: Rowman and Littlefield, 2000.

Brodie, Fawn M. *Thomas Jefferson: An Intimate History.* New York: Norton, 1974.

Cavalli-Sforza, Luigi Luca. *Genes, Peoples and Languages.* Translated by Mark Seielstaad. New York: Northpoint Press, 2000.

Cavalli-Sforza, Luigi Luca, and Francesco Cavalli-Sforza. *The Great Human Diaspora.* Reading, MA: Addison-Wesley, 1995.

Cavalli-Sforza, Luigi Luca, Paolo Menozzi, and Alberto Piazza. *The History and Geography of Human Genes.* Princeton, NJ: Princeton University Press, 1994, abridged paperback edition.

Copi, Irving M. "Essence and Accident." In *Naming, Necessity and Natural Kinds*, edited by Stephen P. Schwartz. Ithaca, NY: Cornell University Press, 1977.

Corcos, Alain. *The Myth of Human Races.* East Lansing: Michigan State University Press, 1997.

Count, Earl W., ed. *This Is Race: An Anthology Selected from the International Literature on the Races of Man.* New York: Henry Schuman, 1950.

Dubinin, N. P. "Race and Contemporary Genetics." In *Race, Science and Society*, edited by Leo Kuper. New York: Columbia University Press, 1975, pp. 68–94.

Dunn, L. C., and Theo Dobzhansky. *Heredity, Race and Society: A Scientific Explanation of Human Difference.* New York: Mentor Books, 1952.

Eze, Emmanuel Chukwudi, ed. *Race and the Enlightenment: A Reader*. Cambridge, MA: Blackwell Publishers, 1997.

Fanon, Frantz. *Black Skin, White Masks*. Translated by Charles Lam Markmann. New York: Grove, 1967.

Fodor, Jerry. "Special Sciences." *Synthese* 28 (1974): 77–113.

Foster, Eugene, M. A. Jobling, P. G. Taylor, P. Donnelly, P. de Knijffs, Rene Mieremet, T. Zerjal, and C. Tyler-Smith. "Jefferson Fathered Slave's Last Child." *Nature* 396 (November 5, 1998): 27–28.

Goodman, Alan, "Six Wrongs of Racial Science." In *Race in 21st Century America*, edited by Curtis Stokes, Theresa Melendez, and Genice Rhodes-Reed. East Lansing: Michigan University Press.

Gordon, Lewis. *Existentia Africana*. New York: Routledge, 2000.

Gould, Stephen Jay. *The Mismeasure of Man*. New York: Norton, 1996.

Hacking, Ian. *The Social Construction of What?* Cambridge, MA: Harvard University Press, 1999.

Hannaford, Ivan. *Race: The History of an Idea in the West*. Baltimore: Johns Hopkins University Press, 1996.

Herrnstein, R. J., and Charles Murray. *The Bell Curve*. New York: The Free Press, 1994.

Hiley, David R. *Philosophy in Question: Essays on a Pyrrhonian Theme*. Chicago: University of Chicago Press, 1988.

Hill, Jason. *Becoming a Cosmopolitan: What It Means to Be a Human Being in the New Millennium*. Lanham, MD: Rowman and Littlefield, 2000.

Hume, David. "Of National Characters." In *Essays Moral, Political and Literary*, 2 vols., edited by T. H. Green and T. H. Grose. London: Longmans, Green and Col, 1875.

———. "Of the Populousness of Ancient Nations." In Green and Grose, *Essays*.

International Human Genome Sequencing Consortium. "Initial Sequencing and Analysis of the Human Genome." *Nature* 409 (February 15, 2001): 860–92.

Jablonski, Nina, and George Chaplin. "The Evolution of Human Skin Coloration." *Journal of Human Evolution* 39, no. 1 (July 2000): 57–106.

Jensen, A. R. *Educability and Group Differences*. New York: Harper and Row, 1973.

Kant, Immanuel. *Anthropology from a Pragmatic Point of View*. Edited by Hans H. Rudnick. Translated by Victor Lyle Dowdell. Carbondale: Southern Illinois University Press, 1996.

———. *Observations on the Feeling of the Beautiful and the Sublime*. Translated by John T. Goldthwait. Berkeley: University of California Press, 1965.

———. "On the Different Races of Man." In *This Is Race: An Anthology Selected from the International Literature on the Races of Man*, edited by Earl W. Count. New York: Henry Schuman, 1950.

Kevles, Daniel J. *In the Name of Eugenics: Genetics and the Uses of Human Heredity*. Berkeley: University of California Press, 1985.

Kitcher, Philip. "Race, Ethnicity, Biology, Culture." In *Racism*, edited by Leonard Harris. New York: Routledge, 1998.

Kuper, Leo. Edited by *Race, Science and Society*. New York: Columbia University Press, 1965.

Lang, Berel. "Metaphysical Racism (Or: Biological Warfare by Other Means)." In *RACE/SEX: Their Sameness, Difference and Interplay*, edited by Naomi Zack. New York: Routledge, 1997.

Lévi-Strauss, Claude. "Race and History." In *Race, Science and Society*, edited by Leo Kuper. New York: Columbia University Press, 1965.

Lewontin, Richard, *The Triple Helix: Gene, Organism and Environment*. Cambridge, MA: Harvard University Press, 2000.

Locke, John. *An Essay Concerning Human Understanding*. Edited by Peter H. Niddich. Oxford, UK: Oxford University Press, 1975.

———. *A Letter Concerning Toleration*. Edited by James H. Tully. Indianapolis, IN: Hackett, 1983.

Mayr, Ernst. *The Growth of Biological Thought*. Cambridge, MA: Belknap Press of Harvard University Press, 1982.

Montagu, Ashley. *The Idea of Race*. Lincoln: University of Nebraska Press, 1965.

———. *Race and IQ: Expanded Edition*. New York: Oxford University Press, 1999.

———, ed. *The Concept of Race*, London: The Free Press of Glencoe, Macmillan, 1994, Blackwell Publishers, 1997.

Mourant, Earnest E. *The Distribution of the Human Blood Groups*. Oxford, UK: Blackwell, 1954.

Popkin, Richard H. *The History of Skepticism from Erasmus to Spinoza*. Berkeley: University of California Press, 1979.

———. "Hume's Racism." In *Philosophy and the Civilizing Arts: Essays Presented to Herbert W. Schneider*, edited by Craig Walton and John P. Anton. Athens: Ohio University Press, 1974.

———. "Hume's Racism." *Philosophical Forum* 9 nos. 2–3, (Winter-Spring, 1977–1978): 211–26.

———, ed. *The Philosophy of the 16th and 17th Centuries*. New York: Free Press, 1966.

Relethford, John H. *Genetics and the Search for Modern Human Origins*. New York: Wiley Liss, 2001.

———. *The Human Species: An Introduction to Biological Anthropology*. Mountain View, CA: Mayfield, 1997, p. 403.

Robins, Ashley H. *Biological Perspectives on Human Pigmentation*. Cambridge UK: Cambridge University Press, 1991.

Root, Maria P. P., ed. *Racially Mixed People in America*. Newbury Park, CA: Sage, 1992.

————, ed. *The Multiracial Experience: Racial Borders as the New Frontier*. Newbury Park, CA: Sage, 1996.

Ruse, Michael. *Philosophy of Biology Today*. Albany: State University of New York Press, 1988.

Schwartz, Stephen P.. Edited by *Naming, Necessity and Natural Kinds*. Ithaca, NY: Cornell University Press, 1997.

Searle, John. *The Construction of Social Reality*. New York: Free Press, 1995.

Smedley, Audrey. *Race in North America: Origin and Evolution of a Worldview*. Boulder, CO: Westview Press, 1999.

Sober, Elliott. "Evolution, Population Thinking and Essentialism." In *Conceptual Issues in Evolutionary Biology*, edited by Elliott Sober. Cambridge, MA: MIT Press, 1997.

Spencer, Ranier. *Spurious Issues: Race and Multiracial Identity Politics in the United States*. Boulder, CO: Westview, 1999.

Tattersfield, Nigel. *The Forgotten Trade*. London: Jonathan Cape, 1991.

Templeton, Alan. "Human Races: A Genetic and Evolutionary Perspective." *American Anthropologist* 100, no. 3 (1998): 632–51.

Weiner, Alexander S. "Anthropological Investigations on the Blood Groups." In *This Is Race: An Anthology Selected from the International Literature on the Races of Man*, edited by Earl W. Count. New York: Henry Schuman, 1950, pp. 679–87.

Wolpoff, Milford, and Rachel Caspari. *Race and Human Evolution*. New York: Simon and Schuster, 1997.

Wolpoff, Milford, John Hawks, and Rachel Caspari, "Multiregionalism, Not Multiple Origins." *American Journal of Physical Anthropology* 112 (2000): 129–36.

Zack, Naomi. *Bachelors of Science: Seventeenth Century Identity, Then and Now*. Philadelphia: Temple University Press, 1996.

————. "Goldberg on Segregation and Prisons." *African Philosophy* 13, no. 2 (2000): pp 164–71.

————. "Lockean Money, Globalism and Indigenism," *Canadian Journal of Philosophy*, 1999 Supplementary Volume 25, Catherine Wilson, ed., *Civilization and Oppression*, Calgary: University of Calgary Press, 1999, pp. 31–53.

————. "Mixed Black and White Race and Public Policy." In *Race, Class, Gender and Sexuality: The Big Questions*, edited by Naomi Zack et al. Malden, MA: Blackwell Publishers, 1998.

————. "Philosophy and Racial Paradigms." *The Journal of Value Inquiry* 33 (1999): 299–317.

————. *Race and Mixed Race*. Philadelphia: Temple University Press, 1993.

————. "Race and Philosophic Meaning." In *Race and Racism*, edited by Bernard Boxill. Oxford, UK: Oxford University Press, 2001, pp. 43–58.

————. *Thinking About Race*. Belmont, CA: Wadsworth, 1998.

————, ed. *RACE/SEX: Their Sameness, Difference and Interplay*. New York: Routledge, 1997.

————, ed. *Women of Color and Philosophy*. Malden, MA: Blackwell Publishers, 2000.

Zack, Naomi, Laurie Shrage, and Crispin Sartwell, eds. *Race, Class, Gender and Sexuality: The Big Questions*. Malden, MA: Blackwell Publishers, 1998.

Index